Cambridge Elements

Elements in Ancient Philosophy
edited by
James Warren
University of Cambridge

VICE IN ANCIENT PHILOSOPHY

Plato and Aristotle on Moral Ignorance and Corruption of Character

Karen Margrethe Nielsen
University of Oxford

CAMBRIDGE
UNIVERSITY PRESS

Shaftesbury Road, Cambridge CB2 8EA, United Kingdom

One Liberty Plaza, 20th Floor, New York, NY 10006, USA

477 Williamstown Road, Port Melbourne, VIC 3207, Australia

314–321, 3rd Floor, Plot 3, Splendor Forum, Jasola District Centre, New Delhi – 110025, India

103 Penang Road, #05–06/07, Visioncrest Commercial, Singapore 238467

Cambridge University Press is part of Cambridge University Press & Assessment, a department of the University of Cambridge.

We share the University's mission to contribute to society through the pursuit of education, learning and research at the highest international levels of excellence.

www.cambridge.org
Information on this title: www.cambridge.org/9781009468039

DOI: 10.1017/9781108581738

When citing this work, please include a reference to the DOI 10.1017/9781108581738

First published 2023

A catalogue record for this publication is available from the British Library.

ISBN 978-1-009-46803-9 Hardback
ISBN 978-1-108-71343-6 Paperback
ISSN 2631-4118 (online)
ISSN 2631-410X (print)

Vice in Ancient Philosophy

Plato and Aristotle on Moral Ignorance and Corruption of Character

Elements in Ancient Philosophy

DOI: 10.1017/9781108581738
First published online: December 2023

Karen Margrethe Nielsen
University of Oxford

Author for correspondence: Karen Margrethe Nielsen, karen.nielsen@philosophy.ox.ac.uk

Abstract: Ancient philosophers offer intriguing accounts of vice – virtue's bad twin. This Element considers injustice and lawlessness in Plato and Aristotle. Starting with Socrates' paradoxical claim that 'tyrants and orators do just about nothing they want to do' (*Gorgias* 466d–e), it examines discussions of moral ignorance and corruption of character in Plato's *Republic* and Aristotle's *Nicomachean Ethics*. Aristotle's account of vice is indebted to Plato's. But his claims have confounded critics. Why is the vicious agent full of regrets when he acts in accordance with his wish? To what extent is vice a form of moral ignorance? Why will the unjust man never get what he wants? These and other questions yield new insights into ancient Greek ethics and moral psychology, as well as surprising perspectives on contemporary debates.

Keywords: vice, Plato, Aristotle, injustice, lawlessness

ISBNs: 9781009468039 (HB), 9781108713436 (PB), 9781108581738 (OC)
ISSNs: 2631-4118 (online), 2631-410X (print)

Contents

1 Desire and Great Power in the *Gorgias*

1.1 Wanting the Good

In Plato's *Gorgias*, a young colt named Polus startles Socrates by declaring that tyrants and orators have the greatest power in the city, since they 'put to death anyone they want, and confiscate the property of anyone they see fit and banish them from their cities' (*Gorgias* 466b). Polus' teacher Gorgias has persuaded him that the greatest good for humankind is 'the ability to persuade by speeches judges in a law court, councillors in a council meeting, and assemblymen in an assembly or in any other political gathering that might take place' (*Gorg*. 452d). With this ability, Gorgias' students will make all men their slaves, including free citizens in democratic assemblies and law courts. The expertise of judges, councillors, or assemblymen is no match for the orator's art. By hook or by crook, the orator can persuade just about anyone of just about anything. The impressionable Polus is already *on* the hook, for like other Athenian young men from aristocratic families, he has been persuaded to spend considerable sums on fees to learn the art of public speaking from Gorgias.[1] Now, Polus wants to convince Socrates that rhetoric grants the orator an enviable power. To be powerful is to live your life according to your own wishes, doing as you see fit, without being constrained. Oratory is the art that secures this freedom, and political power to boot. The successful orator will not just be *like* a tyrant: if all goes well, he will become a tyrant. It seems that Gorgias has broken in his young student successfully.[2]

Polus' paean to the tyrant's life sets off a détente with Socrates over the nature of power and expertise. Socrates seeks to establish a connection between expertise and the good: only someone who knows what to want will get what he wants. Orators and tyrants confuse expertise in getting your heart's desire with expertise in knowing what to desire. As Socrates remarks to Meno, another ambitious young man who has studied with Gorgias, 'what else is misery than desiring bad things and securing them?' (*Meno* 78a). According to Socrates, 'orators and tyrants have the least power in their cities', for 'they do just about nothing they want to do (*ouden gar poiein hōn boulontai hōs epos eipein*), though they

[1] Not all of Gorgias' students were aristocrats: Antisthenes studied rhetoric under him, despite not having Athenian citizenship (his mother was a Thracian or possibly Phrygian slave). Antisthenes later became a follower of Socrates, and the founder of Cynicism.

[2] The first known use of the word *turannos* in Greek literature is a reference to King Gyges of Lydia in a fragment of a poem by Archilochus (680–*c*.645 BC) (fr. 19 West). Thucydides contrasts hereditary kings, who have limits to their power, with tyrants, who were sole rulers with absolute power (Thuc. 1.12.1). Aristotle discusses the causes of tyranny in *Politics* V.10. He notes that almost all tyrants started out as 'demagogues who gained the favor of the people by their accusations of the notables' (1310b15); a few were kings and magistrates who overstepped the limits of their power. For a historic survey of the idea of tyranny, see the introduction to Gwynn (1991).

certainly do whatever they see most fit to do (*poiein mentoi hoti an autois doxēi beltiston einai*)' (*Gorg*. 466d–e).

That doing what you see fit and doing what you want can come apart is not a claim likely to meet with immediate approval. Polus is not impressed. It is not hard to see why: I can list the objects of my desire with some degree of authority – some might say with ultimate authority. If I do as I please – confiscating my enemy's property, banishing him, and putting him to death – it seems that I *have* got what I want, even if I may come to regret it. How might I fail to get what I want even as I do as I please?

To see why, we must attend to the structure of our desires. Let y be an end, and x a means to y. If I want x for the sake of y, then my desire for x is conditional on my desire for y. Socrates notes that acts like sitting, walking, running, and making sea voyages are sometimes good, sometimes bad, depending on the benefit or harm they bring. When we undertake such acts, we do not want the acts for their own sake. Rather, we choose these 'intermediaries' (*ta metaxu*) for the sake of the benefits they bring. When we take medicine, we do not want the act of taking the medicine, with all its discomforts, but rather that for the sake of which we take it, namely, health. Similarly, seafarers do not take dangerous and troublesome sea voyages for the sake of the journey itself, but rather for the sake of making money. In the same way, tyrants and orators do not put people to death, banish them, and confiscate their property for its own sake, but because they assume that they will profit from these actions.[3] To understand why such intermediaries are chosen, we need to know what *purpose* they serve. It is for the sake of the good, claims Socrates, that those who do all these things do them. We put a person to death, and we banish him and confiscate his property because we suppose that doing these things is *better* for us than not doing them (*Gorg*. 468b).[4] Whether it is in fact better, depends on the answer to two questions: (1) is the act an effective means to the end? and (2) is the end itself worth pursuing *because it is good*? If it's the opposite, then for all their skill and cleverness, the tyrant and orator will secure a great evil. If I have a choice between getting what *seems* good to me and what *is in fact* good, I prefer the latter: I want what *appears* good to me because it appears *good*. The good, then, is what we ultimately want. The actions I undertake as means are desired on the assumption that they will help me secure what I ultimately want. If they produce benefit,

[3] Even if we choose an act for its own sake, we choose it *qua* good. The same applies if we choose the action both for itself, and for the consequences (cf. *Republic* II 357b–358a). See *Meno* 77b–78a for Socrates' defence of the claim that no one desires what is bad if they know that they will be harmed by it. For discussion of *Meno* 77b–78a, see Scott (2006, ch. 4).

[4] Socrates assumes that our commitment to the good entails a commitment to what is better when we choose between actions.

I want them. If they cause harm, I don't.[5] If, by doing as I please, I undertake actions that are neither good nor bad, or bad, then I don't want to do the actions I do. But if I do what I don't want to do, am I free and powerful? Superficially, I lead a life in accord with my own desires. But once I examine how my specific desires line up with the end that I ultimately want – to lead a good life – my acts are harmful and counter to my goal.[6] By Gorgias' own admission, rhetoric secures the greatest good for humankind. But if rhetoric cannot tell us what is good, then the craft lacks the ability to tell us how to live.

Now, one might object, and Polus does, that a tyrant or orator who does as he sees fit may have great power despite not doing what he wants. After all, isn't having the power to do as you please good in itself – an aspirational goal? Polus accuses Socrates of secretly craving this power: 'As if *you* wouldn't welcome being in position to do what you see fit in the city, rather than not! As if *you* wouldn't be envious whenever you'd see anyone putting to death some person he saw fit, or confiscating his property or tying him up!' (*Gorg*. 468e). Polus has no reservations about second-guessing Socrates' wishes, which, he claims, are fundamentally like those of tyrants and orators, only suppressed, since he lacks the power to secure the object of his wish. When Socrates says he does not want unlimited power, that's just sour grapes, thinks Polus. It's not in his power to banish and put people to death, but he secretly envies those who can. And if even Socrates envies tyrants and orators, then there's good reason to think that most people do. If, as Mill once observed,[7] the only evidence that something is desirable is that people do in fact desire it, then that settles the question of what is good right there, or so Polus appears to think.

Should we envy the tyrant? Or is he to be pitied for leading an unenviable and miserable life? Polus accuses Socrates of cloaking his impotence in high-minded ideals. If you cannot attain the boundless freedom of orators and tyrants, denying that it has value might produce an ersatz sense of superiority.[8] Conversely, Socrates accuses Polus of holding a flawed conception of power.

[5] This principle underpins Socrates' claim that 'no one errs willingly': I err by choosing acts that won't promote my happiness. Even if I do as I please in choosing my act, I don't want to do acts that will make me miserable. Compare 'you don't want to eat that/go there' spoken to someone about to do just that.

[6] One could object that reflecting on how my desires line up with my ends is not sufficient to determine whether I have good ends. However, Socrates thinks the end I ultimately want is a life that is good, not just a life that I desire. Without qualification, what we want is the good, not what we believe to be good. We will suffer harm if we pursue bad ends, harms that affect the experienced quality of our lives, even if a vicious person may not understand why he is wretched.

[7] Mill (1863, ch. 4), discussed in Crisp (1998) and Sayre-McCord (2011). Socrates and Polus implicitly agree that what we desire is evidence for what is good, but they disagree about what we desire.

[8] Nietzsche's complaints about Socrates echo those Plato puts into the mouths of sophists like Callicles and Thrasymachus. Foot (2001) discusses Nietzsche's debt to Thrasymachus in her final chapter.

If all it takes to have great power is the ability to kill and maim at will, then it is not reserved for the exceptional few, but is available to anyone:

> Imagine me in a crowded marketplace, with a dagger up my sleeve, saying to you, 'Polus, I've just got myself some marvellous tyrannical power. So, if I see fit to have any one of these people you see here put to death right on the spot, to death he'll be put. And if I see fit to have one of them have his head bashed in, bashed in it will be, right away. If I see fit to have his coat ripped apart, ripped it will be. That's how great my power in this city is!' Suppose you didn't believe me, and I showed you the dagger. On seeing it, you'd be likely to say, 'But Socrates, everybody could have great power that way. For this way any house you see fit might be burned down, and so might the dockyards and triremes of the Athenians, and all their ships, both public and private'. But then that's not what having great power is, doing what one sees fit. Or do you think that it is? (*Gorg*. 469d–e)

Carrying a concealed weapon in public confers mighty tyrannical powers on any loser – even a middle-aged, pot-bellied loser like Socrates, who doesn't know how to defend himself in the assembly or in the lawcourt.[9] The power to harm others at will is afforded to anyone in Athens, whether skilled at public speaking or not: it doesn't take a genius to hide a dagger up a sleeve. If power confers superiority, then this isn't it. Polus concedes that 'great power' cannot simply consist in the ability to harm – whether the city's possessions or the citizens themselves. Great power isn't the power to cause harm, but the power to cause harm *while ensuring that no harm comes to oneself.* A person who acts like a thug in the marketplace will necessarily be caught and punished. What distinguishes tyrants and orators from petty criminals is that tyrants and orators have the power to get away with it. For them, the arc of the moral universe bends towards injustice, for the simple reason that they have the power to commit injustice with impunity. Their success is even crowned with official praise and honour: no need for tyrants and orators to hide.

1.2 The Case of Archelaus: Does Injustice Pay?

By conventional standards, being banished, disenfranchised, or executed is harmful *for the victim*.[10] How do such acts affect *the agent*? Suppose a judge imposes the penalty of banishment on a citizen. If the penalty is unjust, Socrates thinks that the judge and the city will be harmed. If it is just, the judge and the

[9] In the *Apology*, Socrates remarks to the jury that he lacks experience speaking in a court of law. He is an accomplished speaker only if an accomplished speaker is one who speaks the truth (see 31e–32a).

[10] Socrates argues in the *Apology* that it is not possible for a worse man to harm a better man, since virtue is sufficient for happiness (30d). He softens his stance in the *The Republic* (II–X), where he instead maintains that virtue is necessary for happiness, and its principal cause.

city will benefit. In keeping with his analysis of *ta metaxu*, Socrates maintains that acts that are neutral in the abstract, will be good or bad for those who do them depending on whether they are just or unjust. By contrast, Polus has ventured that crime – on a large enough scale – pays, since tyrants and orators dominate the docile mob and reap the rewards of injustice without paying a penalty.

To prove that injustice is better for the agent than justice, Polus invokes current affairs: the ascent of King Archelaus of Macedonia. Archelaus was the son of Perdiccas, the ruler of Macedonia, by a slave woman owned by Perdiccas' brother, Alcetas. By law, Archelaus was therefore himself a slave, and the property of his uncle. This bad beginning did not stop Archelaus from rising to power. He first dispatched the legitimate heir to the throne, his master Alcetas, by entertaining him, getting him drunk, and throwing him and his young son Alexander on a wagon to be carried off and slaughtered. He then threw Perdiccas' legitimate son into a well, telling the boy's mother, Cleopatra, that he fell in while chasing a goose and lost his life. Unlike the rogue with a knife in the marketplace, Archelaus is not punished for his crimes. Instead, he is now the King of Macedonia. He can shape the laws however he sees fit, appoint whatever judges he favours, while ensuring that no harm comes to himself. He leads a life of luxury with everyone at his beck and call. Who would not want to enjoy his life?[11] Mocking Socrates' position, Polus declares that it is for this very reason, because he has committed the most terrible crimes of any in Macedonia, that Archelaus 'is now the most "miserable" of all Macedonians instead of the happiest, and no doubt there are some in Athens, beginning with yourself, who'd prefer being any other Macedonian at all to being Archelaus' (*Gorg.* 471c–d). One has to be disingenuous or simple-minded to insist that justice benefits the agent and injustice harms him. Archelaus is supremely unjust and supremely happy.

There is a more unsettling claim waiting in the wings. If justice consists in each person receiving rewards proportionate to his worth, Polus thinks Archelaus deserves to rule: by killing his rivals and neutralizing all opposition, he has proven himself their superior. It is not conventional rules of succession that determine who is fit to rule, and who is fit to serve, but personal qualities like ruthlessness, cunning, and skill, suggests Polus. The conventions of law

[11] The historical Archelaus' press has not been entirely unfavourable, notwithstanding the fact that he gained the throne through murder. During his reign (413–399 BC), he co-operated with Athens (see Thuc. 2.100.2) and championed the arts: Euripides wrote the tragedies *Archelaus* and *Bacchae* as a visitor in his court. Aristotle discusses the causes of his assassination in *Politics* V.10 (1311b4–36). The Cynic philosopher Antisthenes wrote a volume named *Archelaus* which denounced tyranny.

must yield to the force of nature – notwithstanding that Polus thinks he can learn how to be superior from Gorgias.[12]

Socrates doubles down by claiming that Archelaus would be better off if he were punished for his crimes. Getting away with murder only makes his life worse. To Polus' ears, this is preposterous:

> Suppose he is caught, put on the rack, castrated, and has his eyes burned out. Suppose that he is subjected to a host of other abuses of all sorts, and then made to witness his wife and children undergoing the same. In the end he is impaled and tarred. Will he be happier than if he hadn't got caught, had set himself up as a tyrant, and lived out his life ruling his city and doing whatever he liked, a person envied and counted happy by fellow citizens and aliens alike? Is *this* what you say is impossible to refute? (*Gorg*. 473c–d)

To insist that Archelaus would be better off impaled and tarred invites ridicule: no argument can save you if this is a consequence of your position.[13] But Socrates does not relent. If Archelaus plotted to set himself up as a tyrant unjustly, then he will be miserable whether he escapes or is caught and undergoes torture, claims Socrates. Doing what is unjust is far worse than suffering injustice. The person who suffers injustice is affected in his external circumstances, while the person who commits injustice corrupts his own being: vice is corruption of the soul. That type of corruption affects your well-being more profoundly than physical pain and public humiliation. External circumstances are no match for the impact that your internal state has on your well-being. The soul is that by which we live, and hence more important than any other aspect of our being: 'Of two people, each of whom has something bad in either body or soul, which is the more miserable one', asks Socrates, 'the one who is treated and gets rid of the bad thing, or the one who isn't, but keeps it?' (*Gorg*. 478d). Polus has just painted a vivid picture of the badness of physical pain, and so, by his own argument, Polus should concede that in the case of the body, the one who gets rid of badness is better off than the one who keeps it. But the case of the soul is just the same.

To the extent that punishment can rid us of injustice, Socrates thinks we are better off if we pay our dues. If we retain injustice in our souls, it makes no difference whether we are punished or whether we escape. Nothing could exceed or compensate for the badness of having the best part of your being corrupted by injustice, cowardice, ignorance, and the like. Far from being

[12] Later, we learn that Polus has a residual sense of shame: he lacks Archelaus' ruthless natural character. Polus' shame, Callicles complains, makes him vulnerable to refutation.

[13] Polus' claim concerns an unjust man. Contrast Aristotle's claim that a *virtuous* man cannot be happy if he suffers the worst evils and misfortunes (*Nicomachean Ethics* (*NE*) I.5, 1096a3). Aristotle accuses Socrates of defending a 'philosopher's paradox' when he holds that virtue is sufficient for happiness.

trapped in a reductio of his own making, then, Socrates thinks he has reason on his side. The unjust man should not play the coward, thinks Socrates, but rather, like a patient gritting his teeth and presenting himself to the doctor with grace and courage for cauterization and surgery, he should be his own chief accuser: 'If his unjust behaviour merits flogging, he should present himself to be whipped; if it merits imprisonment, to be imprisoned; if a fine, to pay it; if exile, to be exiled; and if execution, to be executed' (*Gorg.* 480d). And he should adopt this attitude, not just to himself, but to friends and family members, so they too can get rid of the worst thing there is, injustice.

1.3 Virtue, Vice and Function

Socrates' exchange with Polus crystallizes Plato's conception of vice: injustice is to the soul what disease is to the body, a disorder that impedes the soul's proper function. It doesn't just harm those who cross paths with the unjust man, but harms the unjust man himself, since the soul is responsible for all his powers and abilities, and allows him to use health, wealth, and other non-moral goods well. A corrupted body causes pain and impedes our activities. But a corrupted soul makes it impossible to live well. In thinking of vice as a corruption of the soul, Socrates treats it as a special instance of a general rule. In the so-called function argument in the *Republic*, Socrates argues from the nature of artefacts, organs, and living beings (*Rep.* I 352d–354a).[14] Consider any substance with a function – whether an artefact or a living being. In each case, its function or characteristic activity is the exercise of the powers because of which the substance is a substance of its kind. If the artefact is in good order, it will work well and benefit its user. If the living being is in good order, it will carry out its characteristic activities well. The lives of citizens will likewise be impeded if they are unjust, claims Socrates. In this case, they will be prevented by their vices from leading a happy life: they cannot be friends to themselves or others. Even if they have an abundant supply of wealth and health and other non-moral goods, they will not use them well, and so they derive no benefit from them unless their souls are in the best state. The tyrant, who is supremely unjust, will be supremely unhappy because of his injustice.

The Greek term *aretē* refers to good character, while *kakia* refers to bad character and badness in general. The associated adjectives *agathos* (good) and *kakos* (bad) describe the goodness or badness of any living thing or artefact.[15] Goodness is the excellent state of x qua x (insofar as it is what it is), and badness

---

[14] This function argument in *Republic* I is bookended in *Republic* X by a parallel argument concerning vice; the 'special badness argument' (609a–611a). Aristotle offers a more worked-out version of the function argument in *EN* I.7, though it has no counterpart in *EN* X.

[15] *Aretē* lacks an adjectival form. The Latin *virtus* is the origin of the English *virtue*, just as *vitium* is the origin of *vice*.

the defective state of x qua x. In living things, vice involves natural corruption, which compromises characteristic life activities: a bad horse is a horse that is bad at the activities that good horses do well. In artefacts, badness likewise involves poor function: a bad pruning knife is a pruning knife that prunes badly. In human bodies, badness consists in disease and disorder, while health and strength are good physical states. In human souls, badness consists in disorder and lack of discipline. In the *Gorgias*, Socrates observes that when a human soul is corrupt (*ponēra*), it is 'foolish (*anoētos*), undisciplined (*akolastos*), unjust (*adikos*) and impious (*anhosios*)' (*Gorg*. 505b). Insofar as human animals are characterized by their rationality, vicious character involves the corruption of the powers of practical rationality that help define the human soul: 'taking care of things, ruling, deliberating and the like' (*Rep*. I 353d). In *Republic* I, Socrates notes that a bad soul rules and takes care of things badly, while a good soul does so well. If justice is the soul's virtue, and injustice its vice, it follows that a just soul will take care of things, deliberate, and rule well, while an unjust soul will do so badly. But since these activities are characteristic of human *life*, a just man will live well, and an unjust man will live badly (*Rep*. I 354a). Socrates assumes that living well is good for us, while we're harmed by living badly. In *Gorgias* 507c, he likewise infers that the completely good person (*agathos anēr teleōs*) who does everything that he does well (*eu*) and admirably (*kalōs*) will be *happy* and blessed because he lives well, and that the corrupt man (*ponēros*), who does badly (*kakōs*), will be *miserable* (*athlios*) on account of the way he lives.[16]

Even if this inference is too quick, Socrates still offers a plausible account of vice as a type of corruption of the soul, akin to disease and disorder in the body.[17] Whether all such corruption amounts to injustice is a further question. Plato and Aristotle both maintain that justice in general is the optimal state of the soul, and that this type of justice entails the other virtues. As Socrates puts it, the just person will also be brave, pious, temperate, and wise: a completely good man. We may still wonder, however, if any deviation from complete goodness is a vice. Just as there's a difference between bubonic plague and a pinched nerve, there is a difference between minor character flaws and all-out vice, one might argue. Some flaws are minor,[18] and though others are major, they needn't

[16] See *Republic* I. In *Republic* II–X, Socrates instead defends a more moderate comparative claim – the just person is always happier than the unjust – since the state of the soul will always control happiness; injustice by making it unattainable, justice by making it attainable. No other good will match the benefit of having the best part of you in an excellent state, and conversely, no other evil will match the harm of having the best part of you – the soul – in the worst possible state.

[17] We do not need to share Socrates' belief in an immaterial separable soul to hold that vice involves a corruption of the capacity for sound normative reasoning and for the execution of our decisions.

[18] For Aristotle, the vicious are not simply people with minor flaws, but for all that, bad people are not all equally bad (see Section 3.5). The Stoics explicitly argue that since all virtues (*virtutes*) are equal (*pares inter se*), so are all vices (*vitia*) (see e.g. Cicero, *Paradoxa Stoicorum*, III.21).

involve ill will or the desire to harm or injure the interests of others. Cowardice, wastefulness, and intemperance are human vices, but they don't involve malice or ill will.[19] Nor is *kakia* the same as sin: a violation of a divine command or divine law. For Plato, with the exception of impiety, vices manifest in the relationship between members of a political community, and only indirectly in the relation between humans and gods.

Plato's terminology mirrors his naturalist account of virtue and vice. We would not call a blunt knife vicious – nor would we call a malfunctioning eye depraved, though we would call them a *bad* knife or a *diseased* eye. By contrast, *kakia* refers to any kind of corruption, regardless of where it obtains. *Ponēria* is equally used across the board (e.g. *Gorg*. 505b about a soul; *Rep*. 609e about the corrupt state of grain, eyes, metals etc), as is *mochthēria*.[20] In the so-called special badness argument for the immortality of the soul (*Rep*. X, 609a–611a), Socrates maintains that there is a badness special to each thing (*oikeion kakon*) that in each case causes it to become corrupted (*mochthēron*): ophthalmia in eyes, disease in the body, blight in grain, rust in iron or bronze, and injustice in a soul. If this special badness (*oikeia ponēria*) doesn't destroy the subject, nothing else will destroy it.[21] But while injustice 'kills other people if it can', it has an invigorating effect on the unjust man: 'on top of making the unjust themselves lively, it even brings them out at night', remarks Glaucon (*Rep*. X 610e). It follows that injustice is very far from being deadly to its possessor. Socrates concludes that since the soul's special vice is not deadly to the soul, it

The same applies to acts, because they upset the rational order: 'Every wrong action throws reason and order into confusion (*perturbatio*), and once reason and order are in confusion, nothing can be added to make the wrong action look more wrong' (III.26). As Cicero explains the Stoic position, crimes that look different in seriousness – killing one's father and killing a slave – are on a par, though in the first case, the killer also commits an act of injustice – perhaps filial impiety – against his father, *in addition* to murder (III.26).

19 We should therefore resist translating *kakia* as 'evil'.

20 The noun *mochthēria* is derived from the verb *mochtheō*, which means to be weary, worn out, or distressed (*mochthēma* means toil or hardship). The *mochthēros* is a base person – someone wretched. In this light, it is perhaps unsurprising that ancient philosophers argue that the wicked man is *miserable*. Plato goes back and forth between using *ponēria*, *kakia*, and *mochthēria* to refer to a corrupted state of any subject (including lack of skill in pilots and sailors (*tēn tōn kubernētōn kai nautōn mochthērian*, *Statesman* 302a). In the 'special badness' argument in *Republic* X, he uses *kakia* and *ponēria* primarily for the *causes* of corruption and *mochthēria* for the corrupt state that results. Some scholars have argued that Aristotle draws a distinction between all-out vice, covered by *kakia*, and the 'ordinary' baseness displayed by hoi polloi, which, they argue, is what Aristotle means when he speaks of the base – *phauloi* – without qualification. For the view that *kakia* in Aristotle denotes a particularly serious form of badness, see Barney (2020), and Warren (2022, ch. 4).

21 In earlier Greek literature, there is no sharp opposition between being *ponēros* and good: any person oppressed by toils is *ponēros*. Heracles is described by Hesiod (Fragments 138, 139) as '*ponērotatos kai aristos*' – the most *wretched* man on account of his madness and subsequent penance, but still the *best* kind of man, since he succeeded in performing the labours.

will never be destroyed, though the human being can die at the hands of others who inflict the death penalty on the unjust.

1.4 "Might Makes Right": Callicles' Challenge

Why should we believe that unjust acts harm the soul, or that this type of harm, if it obtains, isn't a price worth paying to reap the rewards of injustice? It's not clear that being corrupted is always bad for the person whose soul is corrupted, or that it will always make his life more miserable than it would have been, had he not been corrupted. If I commit the perfect crime, I have used my capacity for deliberation and decision for nefarious ends, and to that extent, I am unjust. Like a doctor who uses her expertise to kill, I have enlisted practical reason in the service of injustice. Still, I'm now filthy rich. Socrates makes Polus admit that of two types of corruption – the internal corruption of the soul (*hē tēs psuchēs ponēria*), and the external corruption of the body and of one's finances – poverty and disease are not as bad as injustice. Injustice is worse because it is *more shameful* (*aischiston*) than the other types of corruption, Polus concedes – and this means that it 'surpasses the others by some monstrously great harm, and astounding badness', as Socrates puts it. For this reason, 'injustice (*adikia*), lack of discipline (*akolasia*),[22] and all the other forms of corruption of the soul (*kai hē allē psuchēs ponēria*) are the worst thing there is (*megiston tōn ontōn kakon estin*)' (*Gorg*. 477e).

Revealing his decent upbringing, Polus acknowledges that shame is a fitting response to a soul in a corrupt state. Shame is not simply an emotion that 'dwells in the eyes of others', but an attitude that we are right to assume when we perceive injustice and lack of discipline in ourselves. Because he is a young man, and still prone to shame, his admiration for tyrannical power sits uneasily with his aristocratic ideals. When Socrates exposes the conflict, Polus steps back from the brink. It's a contingent fact that Polus still cares about *honour* as a trait of the character, and not just about public reputation and offices: Socrates' refutation succeeds due to a contingent fact about Polus' values. A young man who has purged any sense of shame from his soul would not give ground so easily. Polus still cares about corruption of character, and takes this to be even more harmful to the person who is corrupted than corruption of the body is harmful to the person who is sick.

---

[22] The terms *sōphrosunē* and *akolasia* are often translated as 'temperance' and 'intemperance', which suggests a straightforward linguistic parallel, though the Greek terms have different roots. *Sōphrōn* is derived from *sōs* (safe, sound) and *phrēn* (mind), and so means *of sound mind*, which in Attic literature came to be associated with being temperate and self-controlled with respect to one's appetites. Aristotle unpacks the meaning of *sōphrosunē* as *'sōdzousan tēn phronēsin'* – the state that preserves *phronēsis* (*EN* VI.5 1140b12–23). *Akolastos* means undisciplined or unbridled (*koladzein* means to correct or chastise). It is sometimes translated 'incorrigible', though that implies that all *akolasia* is incurable, which Aristotle suggests at one point in *EN* VII.8, though he is probably here making a contested point on the basis of etymology.

If Socrates is right that the unjust man is better off if he is punished, then the value of oratory appears to be diminished. The ability to persuade judges in a law court places the unjust man in an even worse predicament than he would be in, had he failed to pervert the course of justice.[23] And if he is able to persuade councilmen in a council or assemblymen in an assembly to approve his unjust plans, then he will mute his critics – the very people who could deliver him from falsehood. When Polus boasts that even a child could refute Socrates and show that what he is saying isn't true (*Gorg*. 470c), Socrates responds that, in that case, 'I'll be grateful to the child, and just as grateful to you if you refute me and rid me of this nonsense' (*Gorg*. 470c). It is a greater good, claims Socrates, to be delivered from falsehood than to deliver others from it. If you are ignorant, you will be worse off if you have the ability to persuade others to accept a falsehood than if you are open to being persuaded to accept a truth. The orator is beholden to his audience, the *demos*, and tells the audience what it wants to hear. The philosopher, who loves wisdom rather than the *demos*, will not indulge his audience by flattering them. Instead, he is beholden to the truth, a far less fickle beloved since it always remains the same.

Alas, Polus is unable to refute Socrates. It is left to the older and wizened Callicles to take Socrates to task for what Callicles thinks is a naïve attitude to persuasion and argument. While Polus may be young and inexperienced, and vulnerable to Socratic refutation, Socrates is himself unmanly, claims Callicles. His earnest pursuit of truth exposes him to harm from those who have power – and especially from the orator. A real man can speak eloquently in the assembly and in a law court, while the philosopher speaks haltingly and plays around like a child. He avoids the centre of the cities and the marketplaces, in which men attain pre-eminence. Instead, he lives his life in hiding, 'whispering in a corner, with three or four boys, never uttering anything well-bred, important, or apt' (*Gorg*. 485e). Ominously warning Socrates of the consequences of his way of life, Callicles remarks that if someone pressed false charges against a philosopher, accusing him of injustice, he could not defend himself. Instead, 'he would feel dizzy, his mouth would hang open, and he would not know what to say'. A philosopher, ventures Callicles, 'is the kind of man one could knock on the jaw without paying what's due for it' (*Gorg*. 486c).[24]

---

[23] As Socrates warns the jurors after his conviction. 'You are wrong if you believe that by killing people you will prevent anyone from reproaching you for not living the right way. To escape such tests is neither possible nor good, but it is best and easiest not to discredit others but to prepare oneself to be as good as possible' (*Apology* 39d).

[24] However, by his own standards, Socrates held his own against his accusers. A. J. Ayer did not pull his punches either: 'As related by Ben Rogers in *A. J. Ayer: A Life*, Ayer – small, frail, slight as a sparrow and then 77 years old – was entertaining a group of models at a New York party when a girl ran in screaming that her friend was being assaulted in a bedroom. The parties

Socrates may protest all he wants that he has justice on his side. In the real world, the strong rule the weak, and while the conventions of society may say that it is unjust for rulers to exploit their subjects, in reality the inferior have no recourse when the norm is violated. If they cannot enforce their claims against those who prevail in assemblies and law courts, this suggests their claims are null and void. Those who are superior will lay down the law for the rest, and this means that they are entitled to a greater share than the inferior, just as the victor in an athletic competition has a right to his prize. By nature, argues Callicles, it is just 'that the superior should take by force what belongs to the inferior, that the better should rule the worse and the more worthy have a greater share than the less worthy' (*Gorg*. 488b). Meritocracy and political realism here enter into an (unholy) alliance: might makes right. Those with superior intelligence in the affairs of the city should rule – and bravery ensures that they will. By Callicles' reckoning, they are entitled to a greater share than the ruled because they have proved themselves to be stronger and more intelligent than their subjects.

1.5 Sōphrosunē: Imposing Order in the Soul

The conversation between Gorgias' admirers and Socrates reveals two radically opposed conceptions of what it means to have great power and what it means for one's life to succeed. Polus and Callicles endorse an agonistic model of the public sphere. Justice does not require that each person gets equal shares of benefits and burdens, but rather that each person receives benefits and burdens *proportionate to his worth*, and we prove our worth by subjugating others. Socrates objects that Callicles fails to pay heed to proportionate equality (*hē isotēs hē geōmetrikē*) (*Gorg*. 508a): this principle orders the universe into a *kosmos*. It produces partnership and friendship, orderliness (*kosmiotēs*), self-discipline (*sōphrosunē*) and justice (*dikaiotēs*), and has great power (*mega dunatai*) among gods and men, ensuring that each receives benefits and honours in proportion to their worth. Where there is no partnership (*koinōnia*), there is no friendship (*philia*), claims Socrates. Instead, there is disorder (*akosmia*) and lack of discipline (*akolasia*). But Callicles only ignores proportionate equality on the assumption that citizens are roughly equal, an assumption he rejects. By nature, the tyrant *deserves* all the wealth and public offices that he can defend, since it's his ability to acquire and preserve wealth and offices that determines

involved turned out to be Mike Tyson and Naomi Campbell. "Do you know who . . . I am?" Tyson asked in disbelief when Ayer urged him to desist: "I'm the heavyweight champion of the world". "And I am the former Wykeham professor of logic", Ayer answered politely. "We are both pre-eminent in our field. I suggest that we talk about this like rational men". So they did, while Campbell slipped away.' ('The Wickedest Man in Oxford', *New York Times*, 20 December 2000).

whether they are rightly his. Vices like ruthlessness, cunning, and, in a word, injustice, turn out to be admirable qualities, while care and concern for others leave us at a competitive disadvantage. Injustice pays, and rightly so, while justice, in the form of respect for fairness and equal shares, is for losers.

How, then, should we live? Callicles' ideal man allows his appetite to grow as large as possible, while ensuring that he has the courage and wisdom (*andreia kai phronēsis*, *Gorg*. 492a) required to satisfy them. His recipe for a happy and successful life is maximal gratification of maximal appetites. What we want isn't to have all our needs met, since, in that case, 'stones and corpses would be happiest', and humans would do well to lead an ascetic life, satisfying only the most necessary desires. Instead, Callicles recommends that we cultivate rich and varied desires, while ensuring that we have the resources to have them satisfied. Those who praise restraint, in the form of temperance and justice, are simply too cowardly to pursue their aim. 'The truth of it, Socrates', claims Callicles, is that 'wantonness, lack of discipline (*akolasia*), and freedom, if available in good supply, are excellence and happiness; as for these other things, these fancy phrases, these contracts of men against nature, they're worthless nonsense' (*Gorg*. 492 c). Laws that prevent us from seeking our heart's desire pervert nature. Living pleasantly, and so happily, consist not in the state of being full, but in experiencing a maximal flow of pleasure through the uninterrupted enjoyment of greater and greater luxuries. Greed (*pleonexia*) is good, while need is bad. Socrates warns that a soul that places no limit on its pursuit of pleasure will never be well-ordered. Its lack of discipline will cause it to violate norms that make community and friendship possible. Although tyrants and orators may initially keep their ambitions and hunger for power under control, the nature of their desire means they will never be content. Nor should he want his desires to be sated – which is what orderliness and self-discipline would entail. Callicles' ideal man must constantly want more to have any prospect of pleasure. The Herculean effort required to feed his gargantuan desires makes him a Sisyphus. Pleasure is not a mind satisfied, but a mind perpetually dissatisfied. The constant need for replenishment reminds Socrates of souls filling leaky jars with sieves in Hades, and of the messy habits of the stone curlew, a bird whose digestive system is never at rest. It's the process of filling up, not the state of being filled, that gives us pleasure, and so we need to cultivate a perpetual need in ourselves to avoid satiation.

The life of Sardanapalus – of luxury and debauchery – is Callicles' ideal.[25] The ruler controls everyone around him, but places no restrictions on himself.

[25] Diodorus (2.27) portrays Sardanapalus as the last King of the Assyrians (7th century BC), drawing on Ctesisas' lost work *Persica*. His life was one of orgies and debauchery. In Greek literature, he became a byword for Persian decadence (an Orientalist trope).

'How could a man be happy if he is enslaved to anyone at all?', asks Callicles. The problem is that the pleasures of Sardanapalus are always mixed with pain, since they depend for their very existence on a need, which is painful. If oratory is expertise in securing what is good, then it can't be expertise in securing the pleasures of Sardanapalus. The good, rather, would seem to involve order and organization, as can be seen from the case of works of art, from house- and shipbuilding and also from the care of the body. In each case, the craftsman places the object of his craft into a certain organization, 'compelling one thing to be suited for another, and to fit to it until the entire object is put together in an organised and orderly way' (*Gorg*. 504a). The same, suggests Socrates, is true of the soul.

What imposes order in a soul? The law, when it is internalized. A soul is well-ordered when it is lawful, claims Socrates, and lawful when it is structured by law. We become law-abiding and lawful when we possess justice and temperance (*sōphrosunē*). By contrast, a soul is in a bad state when it is lawless, and lawlessness is injustice and lack of discipline (*akolasia*). Just as a man with a body in a wretched state should not be permitted by his doctors to fill himself up with lots of very pleasant food and drink, though he has an appetite for them, a man with a corrupt soul should be prevented by law from indulging his appetites, or otherwise become foolish, undisciplined, unjust, and impious. A temperate person, by contrast, will do what is appropriate with respect to both gods and humans: he will be wise, disciplined, just, and pious. Virtue is temperance and good order in the soul, while vice is lack of discipline and disorder in the soul. The former makes us blessed and happy, while the latter makes us miserable and wretched. Callicles' tyrant, who shows no restraint and has no respect for the law, will never get what he wants.

If Socrates is right, temperance or discipline (*sōphrosunē*) makes a soul good, while intemperance or lack of discipline (*akolasia*) makes it bad. But the very idea of temperance as the opposite of lack of discipline with regard to one's appetites suggests that the soul can be divided into that which masters and that which is mastered – a ruler and a ruled, so to speak – that need to be correctly related. Although the *Gorgias* does not argue explicitly for the existence of a rational and non-rational part of the soul, it identifies the functions that Plato in *Republic* IV assigns to the rational and non-rational parts. Just as there are rulers and ruled in the city, there is a ruler and a ruled in the soul. This parallel between city and soul – developed at length in the *Republic* – assumes that one part is a natural ruler and the other a natural subject. We are not temperate if the part that contains appetites is put in charge, which would result if we followed Callicles' advice and allowed our appetites to grow as large as possible. Reason should rule on account of its ability to attain wisdom and to enact its decisions.[26]

It's time to take stock. Plato thinks of vice as a corruption of the soul, which creates disorder and lack of self-mastery. It is caused by the desire to enjoy more than one's fair share of goods that can be divided up among members of a community, which is seen as a sign of one's superiority. Citizens compete for honours, offices, and wealth in a zero-sum game, where some are winners and become rulers, while others lose, and become subjects. This clamour for power and riches is essentially lawless. Plato thinks that only a correctly framed law, and hence a correctly organized society, can impose order in the soul and thereby promote happiness for members of a community. To prevent vices from spreading in the city and taking hold in the soul, we need the right constitution. Only through correctly framed laws can a political community and its members develop the virtues they need to be happy. The alternative, corruption of the constitution, will also corrupt the character of the citizens, making their collective and private lives miserable and wretched.

In the *Republic*, Plato examines the pathologies of disordered constitutions and souls, to explain the nature and origin of vice. The medicine he prescribes – a state ruled by philosophers who have been educated from childhood to promote the common good without a view to their private interests – is fraught with difficulties of its own. My focus will be Plato's diagnosis of the corruption that can come to afflict both the state and the soul. In particular, I will examine his dissection of tyranny – the worst of all possible constitutions and the worst of all possible form of vice.[27]

2 The Tyrant's Vice in the *Republic*

2.1 Why be Just? Socrates on the Paradoxes of Tyranny

Plato's portrait of the tyrant in book IX of the *Republic* marks the culmination of Socrates' defence of the just life.[28] He has been challenged to explain how justice, because of its very self, benefits its possessor and how injustice harms

---

[26] I will not attempt here to track the apparent development of Plato's model of the soul, a topic on which a lot has been written. In earlier Socratic dialogues, the soul is portrayed as rational through and through. Maintaining that 'virtue is knowledge and vice is ignorance', Socrates argues in the *Protagoras* that if we know what we should do, we will act accordingly. He is committed to seeking knowledge through elenctic inquiry, and is prepared to talk to anyone. Even if Plato seems less sanguine about the elenchus' power to turn around unjust souls in the *Republic*, he remains hopeful about its affirmative power in a limited number of cases, namely, for those who retain true beliefs and a sense of shame. See Scott (2020, part I, chs. 4 and 5). For a fresh approach to Socrates' alleged 'intellectualism' in the *Protagoras*, see Kamtekar (2017).

[27] I will not here explore conceptions of vice in Plato's later dialogues. *Sophist* 228b–e, *Timaeus* 86b–87b, and *Laws* IX 863a–864a offer distinctive analyses of vice and ignorance that complicate the picture from the *Gorgias* and *Republic*. For discussion, see Rowe (2020).

[28] A longer version of this section appeared as Nielsen (2019).

them (*Rep*. 367d), and why 'injustice is the worst thing a soul can have in it' and 'justice is the greatest good' (*Rep*. 366e). To explain the effects of justice 'because of its very self', Socrates must determine what justice is – its 'nature and origins' – and thereby show that we always have reason to prefer the just life over the unjust, regardless of the rewards and reputations that follow from being *thought* to be just. Since these rewards are 'simulator accessible',[29] an unjust person can enjoy them in full if he 'creates a façade of illusory virtue' around himself and 'deceives those who come near', while keeping behind the façade 'the greedy and crafty fox of the wise Archilochus', as Adeimantus puts it (*Rep*. 365c).[30] In this way, the unjust man can reap the rewards of complete injustice while enjoying the benefits of a reputation for perfect justice. He gets the best of both worlds, and can even placate the gods with pleasant prayers and sacrifices: stories of Hades won't stay his hand and deter him from committing the 'whole of injustice' (*hē holē adikia*): kidnapping and enslaving the citizens and installing himself as tyrant (*Rep*. 344b–c).

The defence of the just life is cast as a choice: between the life of the perfectly just man with an unearned reputation for the worst injustice, and the life of a perfectly unjust man with an undeserved reputation for perfect justice. To vindicate his claim that 'justice is the greatest good', and 'injustice the worst thing a soul can have in it', Socrates must show that the tyrant is the least happy of all in the city, although he has committed the whole of injustice and secured the maximum amount of power and wealth for himself.

What, exactly, is the psychology of vice for Plato? How should we understand the psychological causes of tyranny, the worst form of vice? This question is complicated, not because Plato omits to present a vivid and terrifying portrait of the tyrant in book IX, but because the tyrant by Plato's own lights is not unlike the rest of us, though he lacks fundamental restraints and a sense of shame. In the absence of such restraints, he pursues the aims that we all wish to pursue, but abandon for fear of the consequences. And yet the tyrant pays a high price for his greed. He is not just wicked, but out of his mind. In the most extreme cases, the tyrant becomes a *beast*, devoid of normative competence: he is incapable of recognizing moral norms, and unable to conform his conduct to moral knowledge.[31] The young tyrant retains vestiges of cognitive competence if madness has not yet driven all sense of shame from his soul. At the start of his

---

[29] Reeve (2012, p. 61).

[30] The fox is *kerdalea kai poikilē* – wily and artful in securing gain (*kerdos*) for himself (see Archilochus 89.5).

[31] The wolf analogy in *Rep*. VIII 565d–566a makes the point. I here assume Brink's analysis of normative competence: 'Normative competence . . . involves a kind of reasons-responsiveness that factors into *cognitive competence* – the ability to recognize moral and criminal norms – and *volitional competence* – the ability to conform one's conduct to this normative knowledge'

political career, his actions conform to his normative beliefs. However, Plato reveals that for all his ingenuity and strength, the tyrant's plan will be frustrated: he will not get what he wants. His greed prevents him from enjoying any of the objects of his desire or deriving satisfaction from them. Eventually, the tyrant is tyrannized by his own appetites – like an addict. Rather than enjoying the greatest freedom and the purest pleasure, the tyrannical soul 'is least likely to do what it wants' (*hēkista poiēsei ha an boulēthēi*), claims Socrates: 'forcibly driven by the stings of a dronish gadfly (*hupo oistrou aei hekomenē biai*)' the tyrant 'will be full of disorder and regret (*tarachēs kai metameleias mestē estai*)' (*Rep.* 577e). His soul is 'full of slavery and unfreedom, with the most decent parts enslaved and with a small part, the maddest and most vicious, as their master' (*Rep.* 577d). He has neither friends nor pleasant pastimes to divert him from the consequences of his ruthless pursuit of power. Instead, he lives in a prison of his own making, 'filled with fears and erotic loves of all kinds' (*Rep.* 579b):

> Even though his soul is really greedy for it, he's the only one in the whole city who can't travel abroad and see the sights that other free people want to see. Instead, he lives like a woman, mostly confined to his own house, and envying any other citizen who happens to travel abroad and see something worthwhile. (*Rep.* 579b)

> A real tyrant is really a slave, compelled to engage in the worst kind of fawning, slavery, and pandering to the worst kind of people. He's so far from satisfying his desires in any way that it is clear – if one happens to know that one must study his whole soul – that he is in the greatest need of most things and truly poor. And, if indeed his state is like that of the city he rules, then, he's full of fear, convulsions, and pains throughout his life. (*Rep.* 579d–e)

> He is inevitably envious, untrustworthy, unjust, friendless, impious, host and nurse to every kind of vice, and . . . his ruling makes him even more so. And because of all of these, he is extremely unfortunate and goes on to make those near him like himself. (*Rep.* 580a)

'Womanly', 'slavish', 'fearful', 'poor': the tyrant's ambition has made him the opposite of the manly, masterly, and fearless person he wants to be. While ostensibly the envy of all his subjects – 'a true man' (*hōs alēthōs anēr*, *Rep.* 359b2) – his life is impoverished by his own injustice. To understand the paradoxes of tyranny, we need to examine the moral psychology of the tyrant, whether he leads a private life, or 'some misfortune provides him with the opportunity to become an actual tyrant' (*Rep.* 578c). Why does the tyrant not get

(Brink 2021, p. 3). While the tyrant can conform his conduct to moral norms whenever that seems expedient, he is not capable of responding to moral reasons as such.

what he wants? Why is he enslaved to his own appetites rather than completely free of restraint? How does the tyrant's 'erotic love' differ from the appetites of his subjects? When Plato says that the tyrant is 'forcibly driven by the stings of a dronish gadfly (*oistros*)',[32] how should we understand this 'great winged drone' (*hupopteron kai megan kēphēna*, *Rep.* 573a1) and the painful sting it inflicts on the tyrant's soul?

Despite Polus' fawning admiration for powerful men like Archelaus, his life will be frustrated if he follows in their path. Polus argued that the unjust man is happy, provided he gets away with the 'whole of injustice', in Thrasymachus' words from *Republic* I. It is precisely *because* he has committed the whole of injustice that he is now the happiest of all. If we believe Glaucon's argument concerning Gyges' ring (*Rep.* II 359c–360d), we would all want to follow Archelaus down the path of injustice.[33] But because we are too weak to commit injustice with impunity, we create laws and enter into covenants that prevent us from committing injustice in exchange for protection against others' overreaching. By contrast, the tyrant is lawless (*paranomos*, *Rep.* VII 539a; cf. IX). He overreaches not just because he wants the pleasures and luxuries, but also to mark his superiority by violating norms and laws that bind those who are weak. Justice is for little people – those who lack the power and cunning to get away with the worst type of injustice. Thrasymachus has argued that justice is the good of another, the advantage of the stronger, and 'high-minded simplicity' (*panu gennaian euētheian*, *Rep.* 348e). Those who obey the law are high-minded because they make a virtue of necessity. Their commitment to justice and fairness plays into the hands of the rulers.

---

32 The *oistros* is a stinging gadfly, but is used as a metaphor for any sting that drives someone mad (Euripides, *Hercules Furens* 862), and so for any vehement desire or mad passion (see e.g. Herodotus 2.93 and Euripides *Hippolytus* I 300, as well as Plato *Rep.* 577e). Socrates' sting ideally creates a mad passion (*erōs*) for philosophy. In modern translations, starting with Jowett (1871), Socrates is thought to compare himself in the Apology to a gadfly, an insect related to the *oistros*. This requires taking *muōps* in the same sense as, for example, Aristotle uses it in the *History of Animals*, where he compares the two species. But Laura Marshall has recently presented an intriguing argument for thinking that *muōps* in context means spur – hence its ability to awake the slumbering horse (Athens). See the parallels examined in Marshall (2017).

33 The thought experiment is helpfully discussed by Irwin (1995, ch. 2). Contrast the seeming morale of the story of Gyges' ring as related by Glaucon with the attitude expressed by the poet Archilochus (fr. 19 West), who protests that all the gold of Gyges is of no concern to him, and that he has no love of tyranny:

> The possessions of Gyges rich in gold are of no concern to me,
> not yet have I been seized with jealousy of him, I do not envy
> the deeds of the gods, and I have no love of tyranny.
> That is beyond my sights (Gerber 1999, p. 93).

According to Aristotle (*Rhetoric* III.17, 1418b), Archilochus put these words into the mouth of the carpenter Charon. For an exploration of Archilochus' sources and his use of the Gyges story, see Strauss Clay (1986).

2.2 Human Nature Examined

Vice for Plato is a character trait that comes in multiple varieties, each kind representing a falling away from the harmonious ordering that characterizes the just man and the just state. Plato concedes that the subjects in a well-ordered state will fall short of the virtue displayed by their wise rulers, but denies that this deficiency is a vice.[34] The difference consists in their relation to the good: subjects who respect the laws in a well-ordered state will not themselves possess the wisdom to understand why these laws are just, but they will have true beliefs, and will, to that extent, possess the virtues appropriate for subjects.

Vice, by contrast, involves a pernicious form of ignorance, where false beliefs about the end fill the gap and lead the agent to undertake acts that are harmful to the city and the soul. This ignorance results when non-rational desires and emotions are not restrained by reason. When passions rule, reason cannot perform its natural tasks well: grasping the truth and governing the whole soul in light of its wisdom. This corruption – which produces false beliefs – has internal psychological causes, as well as external social enabling conditions, in the form of household and state dysfunction. The tyrant's vice is the ultimate expression of human nature unchecked by law, whether in its external manifestation in the constitution or its internal manifestations in the soul.[35] These psychological tendencies exist independently of the political circumstances that allow the tyrannical man to ascend to power as a self-appointed champion of the people. Indeed, Plato maintains that lawless desires are not restricted to tyrants: they are present in everyone. Human nature is inherently pleonectic, but at the same time capable of rational governance.[36] Whether our innate pull towards lawlessness or our natural desire for truth ends up setting our course depends on our external circumstances as well as our own efforts. Plato observes that 'some of our unnecessary pleasures and desires are lawless (*tōn mē anankaiōn hēdonōn te kai epithumiōn dokousi tines moi einai paranomoi*)' (*Rep.* IX 571b4–5). He observes that 'they are probably present in everyone, but they are held in check

[34] Thus, the non-philosophers in Plato's ideal state are not just, since they lack wisdom, but they aren't unjust either, since they retain true beliefs.

[35] See the conclusion of *Republic* book IX, where Socrates discusses the internalization of law in the soul as a precondition for freedom. He observes that 'it isn't to harm the slave that we say he must be ruled, which is what Thrasymachus thought to be true of all subjects, but because it is better for everyone to be ruled by divine reason, preferably within himself and his own, otherwise imposed from without, so that as far as possible all will be alike and friends, governed by the same thing . . . This is clearly the aim of the law, which is the ally of everyone' (*Rep.* IX 590c–d). See further Plato's remarks about how the law should be internalized in his discussion of moral education in *Laws* I (e.g. 643a–645a, especially the allegory of the puppets), perceptively analysed in Nightingale (1999). The importance of lawfulness in the just state is explored by Annas (2017).

[36] Plato thus posits an intrinsic tension in human nature, which can be eased through wisdom and wise governance, though the potential for stasis remains.

by the laws and the better desires in alliance with reason' (*Rep.* IX 571b5–7). In a few, godlike people, lawless desires have been eliminated entirely (*Rep.* IX 571b7–9), while in others, only a few weak ones remain. The former include the incorruptible people that Glaucon has in mind in *Republic* book II, when he qualifies his earlier claim that *no one* is willingly just 'apart from someone of a godlike character who is disgusted by injustice or one who has gained knowledge and avoids injustice for that reason' (*Rep.* II 366c). But such people are few and far between: they are either divine or philosopher kings or queens. And so most people – even the best – will have some lawless desires latent in their souls. These desires are awakened in sleep, when the rest of the soul – the rational, gentle, and ruling part – slumbers. Then the 'beastly and savage part, full of food and drink, casts off sleep, and seeks to find a way to gratify itself'. At such a time, 'there is nothing that it dares not do – free of all control by shame or reason' (*Rep.* IX 571c). The appetitive part doesn't shrink from having sex with anyone, whether man, god, or beast – or even a mother. It is wholly without restraint, both in the object of its pursuit and its choice of means.

The only thing that stands between us and the tyrant is the wakefulness of reason and the restrictions imposed by law. That is why someone who wishes to be healthy and moderate should exercise proper sleep hygiene. Before he turns in, he should 'rouse his rational part and feast it on fine arguments and speculations'. He should neither starve nor feast his appetites, so they remain quiet and won't disturb reason with their pleasures and pains. He should soothe the spirited part in the same way, for instance by not turning in while angry. Appetite and spirit need to be quieted and reason roused – that's the only way to ensure that our dreams aren't lawless and that the soul sees the truth in its dreams. For the tyrant, there is no respite. He becomes while awake what he used to become occasionally while asleep (*Rep.* IX 574e). This happens when idlers in the household chase out any remnant of their father's thrift, and the drone they have implanted in his soul – his lazy desire for pleasure – acquires a sting:

> When the other desires – filled with incense, myrrh, wreaths, wine, and the other pleasures found in their company – buzz about (*bombousai*) the drone (*kēphēn*) [the leader in the soul], nurturing it and making it grow as large as possible, they plant the seed of longing in it. Then this leader of the soul (*ho prostatēs tēs psuchēs*) adopts madness as its bodyguard and becomes frenzied. If it finds any beliefs or desires in the man that are thought to be good or that still have some shame, it destroys them and throws them out, until it's purged him of moderation (*heōs an kathērēi sōphrōsunēs*) and filled him with imported madness (*mania*). (*Rep.* IX 573a–b)

The drone is a 'leader of the soul' – it is put in position of ruler by the swarm of appetites and in turn whips the appetites up into a frenzy, much as a leader of a democratic mob stirs the crowd into action and kills his enemies. The use of '*prostatēs*' suggests that the drone represents the leading part of the soul – reason – when it adopts indiscriminate and maximal satisfaction of appetitive desires as its principle. Any desire and any belief that opposes the supremacy of this principle is destroyed and expelled. In the absence of any true belief, madness – in the sense of the deepest illusion about the good – protects the rule of the drone.

Once the traditional opinions that he has held from childhood about what is fine or shameful have been purged from the soul, the lawless desires in the appetitive part are free to seek enjoyment indiscriminately. The tyrannical son uses deceit and force to acquire wealth from any source, lest he suffer greatly from the pain of unfilled cravings. Observing the young tyrant, Plato notes that 'just as the pleasures that are latecomers outdo (*pleon eichon*) the older ones and steal away their satisfactions, won't the man himself think that he deserves to outdo (*pleon eichein*) his father and mother, even though he is younger than they are – to take and spend his father's wealth when he has spent his own share' (*Rep*. IX 574a). If they won't give it to him, he will steal it by deceitful means, and if that doesn't work, he will seize it by force.

How do these 'lawless' desires relate to what Glaucon in *Republic* book II posited as the basic inclination of mankind, namely *pleonexia*? In book II, Glaucon, playing devil's advocate, sought to prove that no one does justice willingly, but only because they are too weak to do injustice with impunity. Justice is like bad tasting medicine: we only obey the laws because we lack the power to do injustice without paying the penalty.

Glaucon says that we will see this most clearly if we grant a just and an unjust person the freedom to do whatever they like: we can then follow both of them and see where their desires will lead. We will catch the just person red-handed, travelling down the same road as the unjust. The reason for this, says Glaucon, is: 'the desire to outdo others and get more and more (*pleonexia*). That's what everyone's nature naturally pursues as good, but nature is forced by law into the perversion of treating fairness with respect' (*Rep*. II 359c).

Pleonexia is not simply greed, if by 'greed' we mean acquisitiveness. It is a kind of greed that does not just want to maximize the good for itself, but to do so at other's expense, in defiance of fairness. It thus arises in matters of distribution, where proportionate equality is at stake. That is why 'the desire to outdo others and get more and more' is an apt explication of the Greek term. The thought that the desire to get more and more and to outdo others is fundamental to human psychology may seem to paint a bleak picture of humanity. It is a conception that is rooted in the Greek notion of justice as 'benefiting one's friends *and harming one's enemies*' (*Rep*. I 332a) with the only exception being that to the pleonectic man, there are no true friends, only real or potential enemies. If this is right, we are by nature not just greedy, but competitive. We don't just want to 'get more and more', but we also want to outdo others. That is, we desire to have more than our fair share of divisible benefits while shirking our fair share of burdens. Thus, we all struggle to get to the top, and seek the maximal satisfaction of maximal desires.

Interestingly, nowhere in the *Republic* does Socrates challenge Glaucon's assumption about human *pleonexia*, but rather takes it for granted that this is, as it were, the default psychology of humankind in the absence of law. At the same time, he holds that 'every soul pursues the good and does whatever it does for its sake' (*Rep*. VI 505e). While many people pursue 'what merely seems just and beautiful, but isn't really so', and 'act, acquire and form their own beliefs' on the basis of how things seem to them, no one, claims Socrates, is content to acquire what merely seems good (*ta dokounta agatha*), but 'everyone wants the things that really are good (*alla ta onta zētousin*), and disdains mere belief here' (*Rep*. VI 505d). While the appetitive part has a pleonectic conception of the good, and seeks to outdo others and have more and more, this objective is not one that will ever lead them to acquire what they truly want. That requires restraint and order, and a reorientation of the soul towards the form of the good. But though perfectly rational philosophers will have tamed the beast within, pleonectic desires are still lurking in their souls, otherwise the proscription of private property would be unnecessary: philosophers would be completely immune to the charms of Gyges' ring. As it is, Plato thinks that 'our dreams make it clear that there is a dangerous, wild, and lawless form of desire in everyone (*deinon ti kai agrion kai anomon epithumiōn eidos hekastōi enesti*), even in those of us who seem to be entirely moderate and measured' (*Rep*. IX 572b). Unless our desires are mastered by reason, which grasps the nature of the good, and orients us towards it, our desires will be at war with what we most fundamentally want.

2.3 Pleonexia: Greed or the Desire to Outdo Others?

In *Republic* book VIII, Socrates clarifies a distinction that had surfaced already on the foundation of the 'healthy' and 'fevered' cities in book II between necessary and non-necessary desires and pleasures: those appetites we (1) can't desist from and (2) whose satisfaction benefit us are necessary, since we are 'by nature compelled to satisfy them' (*Rep*. VIII 558d). Those we could get rid of if we practised from youth are non-necessary provided that their presence leads to no good or the opposite.

The desire to eat to the point of health and well-being is natural and necessary. Bread, for instance, is natural and necessary on both counts: it's beneficial, and unless the desire for bread is satisfied, we die. Delicacies are necessary, to the extent that enjoying them is beneficial and promotes our well-being. The denizens of the city of pigs do not lead a joyless life, but enjoy measured pleasures. As Socrates describes them, they 'put their honest cakes and loaves on reeds or clean leaves, and, reclining on beds strewn with yew and myrtle, they feast with their children, drink their wine, and crowned with wreaths, hymn the gods. They enjoy sex with one another but bear no more children than their resources allow, lest they fall into either poverty or war' (*Rep.* II 372b–c). This lifestyle is sustainable, and does not lead to disease or competition for resources. It is also utterly unrealistic for people like us. Our inborn *pleonexia* makes us seek pleasures that harm both the body and reason and moderation of the soul. Thus, the cravings of actual people are for non-necessary pleasures. In the city with a fever, the citizens do not live in peace and good health, for they their desire for 'all sorts of delicacies, perfumed oils, incense, prostitutes and pastries' (*Rep.* II 373a). Their enjoyment of prostitutes and pastries, together with a new-found love of meat, create a greater need for doctors than before, and so the city with a fever fills up with a class of professional citizens catering to the needs of the fevered population: beauticians, poets, choral dancers, chefs, cooks, and swineherds.[37] To finance their indulgence, the citizens 'surrender themselves to the endless acquisition of money' and 'overstep the limit of their necessities' (*Rep.* II 373d). This leads to wars of aggression: the rapacious city will wage war against neighbouring states to acquire more territory. The appetitive desires that lead to the pursuit of luxuries are highly specific versions of natural desires for food, sex, and drink: Syracusean cuisine, Sicilian-style dishes, and Corinthian girlfriends,[38] to name a few of the delights that Socrates proscribes for trainee guardians (*Rep.* III 404d). Such non-necessary desires could be restrained without hurting our chances of leading a healthy and fulfilled life. Indeed, we would be better off without them.[39]

In book IX, Plato further subdivides the non-necessary desires into lawful and lawless kinds. Lawless desires are not just desires for things that threaten

37 The list overlaps with the practitioners of 'knacks' that Socrates criticizes in the *Gorgias*, whose only skill is flattering the senses. Since they lack any understanding of the good, and aim to please rather than benefit, what they practise falls short of craft (*technē*). See *Gorgias* 463a–465e.

38 The Corinthians were said to practice sacred prostitution at the Temple of Aphrodite (see e.g. the remarks in Strabo 8.6.20; 12.3.36). Plato likely uses the term '*Korinthia korē*' in a loose sense, to denote a female companion (*hetaira*) in a semi-permanent sexual relationship, not to be confused with a simple prostitute (*pornē*).

39 The transition from the 'city of pigs' to the 'luxurious city' in *Republic* book II has struck readers as gratuitous. Why not focus on a healthy city when trying to determine the nature of political justice? The reason is realism: we are not psychologically simple like the modest denizens of the healthy city. As citizens of a real rather than an ideal community, we crave more than satisfaction of our natural and necessary desires. And so Socrates and Glaucon abandon the 'true city' and turn to the city with a fever. Plato is not legislating for ideal citizens: his ideal state is the best state for non-ideal people.

the health of our body and the moderation of our soul, but specifically for things that are shameful in themselves by breaking fundamental norms and conventions. Although Plato does not offer a firm criterion for when a desire counts as lawless, his examples are evocative and suggest that lawless desires are desires for incest, cannibalism, murder, and other proscribed activities. Sleeping with one's mother, or seeking satisfaction with anyone else at all, whether man, beast, or god, is lawless, as is foul murder and consumption of forbidden food and drink – like human flesh or blood.

Such desires are the ones that Aristotle classifies as beastly in *Nicomachean Ethics* VII.5, not because they cannot be resisted – Aristotle envisions that a beastly character like the tyrant Phalaris of Acragas could restrain his desire to eat a child or for some unnatural sexual pleasure (*EN* VII.5 1149a14–16) – but because these desires are *unnatural* in addition to being non-necessary. We do not have to agree with Aristotle's exact list to understand the underlying thought – he throws sex between males in with cannibalism and trichotillomania – nor do we have to agree with his criterion for calling a state or condition bestial. It is still possible to discern a general principle underlying his categorization. In each case, the desire in question is one that arises through disease, bad habits, or congenital conditions that run counter to the norms of nature.[40] Lawless desires, as Plato describes them, break apart social bonds and create enmity and strife in the city by making the citizens pursue satisfaction indiscriminately and in defiance of norms. But unlike Aristotle, Plato takes such paranomic desires to be part of normal human psychology – 'they are probably present in everyone, but they are held in check by the laws and by the better desires in alliance with reason' (*Rep.* IX 571b). This prevents them from becoming manifest in action. Lawless non-necessary pleasures aren't simply excessive, since deriving excessive or highly refined pleasure from food, sex, or drink still involves objects that are natural for human beings. They are rather derived from acts or objects that are shameful and lawless in themselves. There's no such thing as sleeping with your mother at the right time, in the right way, for the right result, to paraphrase Aristotle. In each case, pursuing lawless pleasures means transgressing natural boundaries. If we believe Plato, that's an impulse that lurks deep in the souls even of law-abiding citizens.

How does the greed displayed by the denizens of the fevered city turn into the lawless desires of the tyrant? To answer this question, we need to understand how indulging our limitless desire for unnecessary pleasures unleashes a tyrannical pursuit of lawless and unnatural pleasures. The 'limitless' nature

[40] For an incisive discussion of Aristotle's remarks about bestiality, see Pearson (2018). Kontos (2018) maintains that Aristotle's account of bestiality in *EN* VII.5 contains an endorsement of what he calls 'radical evil', a claim that hinges on Kontos' definition of 'radical evil'.

of non-necessary desires suggests that they cannot be satisfied.[41] Indeed, on Callicles' conception of the appetites, satisfaction of all desires would put an end to enjoyment, and so the tyrant will cultivate desires, allowing his appetites to grow as large and numerous as possible while ensuring that he has the power to satisfy them (*Gorg*. 491e). Once released from restraint, appetitive desires are, in a word, restless.

This restlessness manifests as a search for new and increasingly bizarre sources of pleasure: ones that exceed past sources in intensity and duration. In the case of the emerging tyrant, Plato notes that 'pleasures that are latecomers outdo the older ones and steal away their satisfactions' (*Rep*. XI 574a). Those who indulge their non-necessary appetites will quickly adapt, and need new thrills to experience the pleasure they crave, since old sources no longer deliver. It's not just individual people who 'outdo' each other, in other words, but also pleasures themselves. Plato thus discerns an internal dynamic that leads us to seek new objects of enjoyment in place of old, and where the pursuit of gratification leads us from necessary and healthy delicacies, to unnecessary ones, and eventually to the pursuit of lawless pleasures. In the absence of rational restraint and a sense of shame, we will start enjoying objects that are neither necessary nor natural for human beings. This suggests that human *pleonexia* has the potential to take us all the way to the tyrant's lawless life.

It is instructive at this point to contrast Plato's pleonectic account of human nature with Thomas Hobbes' account of human desire in *Leviathan*. Hobbes (1996) 'puts for the general inclination of all mankind a perpetuall and restlesse desire of Power after power, that ceaseth onely in death' – where the power of man is 'his present means, to obtain some future apparent Good' (p. 70; ch. X, 'Of Power, Worth, Dignity, Honour, and Worthinesse'). While Hobbes' account of the nature and origins of justice resembles Glaucon's in *Republic* II, his analysis of this 'perpetuall and restlesse desire' diverges subtly from Plato's analysis of human nature.[42] First, Plato thinks that reason can tame our appetites, even if they will always remain a potential source of sedition. Hobbes denies that reason is a source of motivation in its own right, and that desire can ever be tamed. Moreover, he does not portray greed as a desire to outdo others, but rather as a means to an end. In chapter 11 of the first part of *Leviathan* ('On Man'), Hobbes rejects the idea that human desire can ever be satisfied, which

[41] Not only are non-necessary desires limitless because the body and its needs continue to require attention, but because if we do not take pleasure in moderation, we will soon derive diminishing pleasures from the same sources, and seek greater and more intense sources of pleasure. In this respect, Plato is right to attribute the desire for money to the appetitive part of the soul.

[42] Hobbes may also have been inspired by Thucydides – he published the first complete translation into English of Thucydides' *History of the Pelopponesian War* (1628). For discussion, see Hoekstra (2015).

certainly seems like an acknowledgement that we are pleonectic. But Hobbes' explanation for why we seek more and more powers (broadly speaking) differs from Glaucon's:

> the Felicity of this life, consisteth not in the repose of a mind satisfied. For there is no such Finis ultimus (utmost ayme,) nor Summum Bonum, (greatest Good,) as is spoken of in the Books of the old Morall Philosophers. Nor can a man any more live, whose Desires are at an end, than he, whose Senses and Imaginations are at a stand. Felicity is a continuall progresse of the desire, from one object to another, the attaining of the former, being still but the way to the later. The cause whereof is, That the object of mans desire, is not to enjoy once onely, and for one instant of time; but to assure for ever, the way of his future desire . . . So that I put for the generall inclination of all mankind, a perpetuall and restlesse desire of Power after power, that ceaseth onely in Death. And the cause of this, is not always that a man hopes for a more intensive delight, that he has already attained to; or that he cannot be content with a moderate power: but because he cannot assure the power and means to live well, which he hath present, without the acquisition of more. (Hobbes 1996, p. 70)

To Hobbes' mind, then, human acquisitiveness and ambition is not a sign that we seek to 'outdo others and get more and more', as Glaucon posits, but rather an expression of the fear that we shall not have quiet enjoyment of the powers that we already have. In short, we lack assurance for the future. People in the state of nature reason like Plato's oligarch, hoarding resources as a bulwark against an uncertain future. Had they been assured of future enjoyment, they could have been content with a 'moderate power'. But since they can't secure the means to live well, their desires will be 'perpetuall and restlesse', argues Hobbes. To Plato's mind, we all seek more and more because we want to do better than our fellow citizens, not because we fear we will lose what little we have.

The competitive aspect of *pleonexia* and its drive towards pre-eminence plays a crucial part in the emergence of the tyrant. While his pursuit of appetitive pleasure drives the budding tyrant to burn through his parent's wealth, and while the need for money makes him break the law, the tyrant's lawbreaking is not primarily instrumental. For the tyrant, breaking the law and casting off all norms and conventions that restrain him is a way of asserting his power, and so to rise above everyone else – citizens he considers competitors in the pursuit of power. The tyrant is driven by appetites strengthened by *erōs* and madness but, unlike his father, the democratic man, he would not be content to have his appetites fully catered for, since that is, in principle if not always in practice, compatible with leaving as much and as good for others. To the tyrant's mind, any restriction on his greed is an affront: a sign that he is not yet supreme. It is only when he is above the law – a rule-maker rather than a rule-taker – that the tyrant will have achieved the complete freedom from restraint that to his tyrannical mind makes him 'like a God among humans', not subject to the laws that, according to Thrasymachus, make the lives of the ruled wretched.

2.4 The Genealogy of Vice

At this point, we should examine the tyrant's genealogy. The tyrant is the fifth generation in a family in decline, each son displaying a character that is inferior to that of his father. These increasingly corrupted characters reflect the shortcomings of earlier generations, as well as the misfortunes suffered by them in the city. They also reflect the social conditions in the city: the presence of strife and enmity, or the presence of a class of corrupting idlers – 'drones' as Plato calls them.

Having concluded the provisional analysis of justice as inner harmony at the end of *Republic* book IV, Socrates observes that this should occasion an inquiry into 'how many forms of vice there are'. 'From the vantage point we've reached in our argument, it seems to me that there is one form of virtue and an unlimited number of forms of vice, four of which are worth mentioning' (*Rep.* IV 445c). Since 'it seems likely' that there are 'as many types of soul as there are specific forms of political constitutions' – namely, five souls and five constitutions – they must study each in turn, starting with the best.

The analysis is delayed, however, while Socrates defends his radical proposals for the guardian's education in books V–VII, and only picked up again at the start of book VIII. The best constitution is the one ruled by one outstanding person or a group of outstanding people: kingship or aristocracy. If this is the correct form of government, all the others are deficient in some way. In descending order, the vicious constitutions and the vicious character states are timocracy and the timocrat, oligarchy and the oligarchic man, democracy and the democratic man, and tyranny and the tyrant. The tyrant, who embodies the worst kind of vice, is thus at the end of a sliding scale of depravity. Aristotle echoes Plato's sentiment about the multiplicity of vice and the singularity of virtue.[43] However, Plato differs from Aristotle in thinking of vices as types of constitutions rather than excessive or deficient states flanking the virtuous mean. Whereas Plato emphasizes different types of rule that can be displayed by a soul, and hence different types of relations between the rational and non-rational soul parts and their respective powers, Aristotle builds his account of

[43] Aristotle remarks that 'there are many ways to be in error – for badness is proper to the indeterminate, as the Pythagoreans pictured it, and good to the determinate. But there is only one way to be correct . . . "for we are noble in only one way, but bad in all sorts of ways"' (*EN* II.6 1106b30–5). Aristotle criticizes Plato in *Politics* V.12 for holding that there's a determinate order in which one character and one constitution devolves into another (1316a18–34).

virtue as an intermediate state (*mesotēs*) that hits what is mean (*to meson*) in action and passion (*EN* II 1106b27–8). Like Plato, Aristotle takes all vice to involve a failure to grasp what is good and why. But importantly, Aristotle holds that there is a right way to relate to the emotions and the subject matter (*peri ho*) of each virtue. By contrast, there is no virtuous mean of the desires that characterize the worst form of Platonic vice. These are lawless desires that are unnatural and unnecessary. Because the worst kind of vice for Plato involves lawless desires, there is no appropriate way of enjoying their satisfaction, and so – by Aristotelian standards – no virtuous mean of which tyranny would be the excessive state.

Plato identifies different psychopathological causes for each of the steps of the descent into tyranny. There may be an unlimited number of forms of vice, but the causes of discrete kinds are still intelligible and amenable to classification. Virtue – in the form of justice – is rule by reason, and vice the corruption of rational rule.[44]

This corruption of reason starts with the appearance of the timocrat, a lover of physical training and hunting, as well as exploits in war. He is the son of an aristocrat in a city that isn't well governed, and ends up torn between the influence of his father and the rest of the household, which pulls him away from moderation and virtue. His aristocratic father leads a private life and doesn't fight back when he is insulted, whether in private or in public in the courts. As a result, he is put at a disadvantage. The timocrat's ambitious mother is angered by her husband's diffidence and blames him for it: 'she tells her son that his father is unmanly, too easy-going, and all the other things that women repeat over and over again in such cases' (*Rep.* VIII 549d). As a result, the timocrat is pulled in contrary directions: 'His father nourishes the rational part of his soul and makes it grow; the others nourish the spirited and appetitive parts' (*Rep.* VIII 550b). What the timocrat comes to realize is that 'those in the city who do their own work are called fools and held to be of little account' (*Rep.* VIII 550b), and so he starts craving money as a means to self-assertion. Since he is not a bad man by nature, but merely keeps bad company, he settles in the middle, and surrenders the rule of himself to the middle part – the victory-loving and spirited part. He becomes honour loving and proud, and subordinates the search for truth to a spirited pursuit of positions of high office. However, whether we achieve or retain high office depends more on those who confer such honours than those on which they are conferred, and so a fundamentally

[44] Annas (2017) aptly observes that the decline of the virtuous person into a timocrat, oligarch, democrat, and tyrant involves a progressive rejection of law, culminating in the tyrant's lawlessness (pp. 15–16). 'Law' includes *nomima*, conventions about decent behaviour that aren't included in written law codes.

decent timocrat will eventually 'crash against the city like a ship against a reef, spilling out all his possessions, even his life' (*Rep*. VIII 553a).

The oligarch is the timocrat's son. He watches with alarm as his father suffers a reversal of fortune. The mature timocrat sticks to his principles despite public disapproval, placing honour above all else. When his enemies bear false witness against him in court, he ends up put to death or exiled or disenfranchised. The oligarch, at first inclined to follow in his father's footsteps, now sees him lose everything: 'humbled by poverty, he turns greedily to making money, and, little by little, saving and working, he amasses property' (*Rep*. VIII 553b). The oligarch desires money, not as a means to the satisfaction of his desires, but rather as an insurance policy against the vicissitudes of fortune. He 'places the appetitive and money-making part on the throne, setting it up as a great king within himself, adorning it with golden tiaras and collars and girding it with Persian swords' (*Rep*. VIII 553c), not because he seeks pleasure from the satisfaction of his appetitive desires, which he seeks to keep minimal and subordinate to the overarching goal of amassing wealth. The oligarchic man is a miser; he wants money for the power and security that it represents when it remains unspent, not for the pleasure it secures when squandered.

In this regard, the oligarchic man and his son, the democrat, are both governed by their appetites, but in different ways. The oligarch is a fearful man, he makes a profit from everything and hoards it, and keeps his 'dronish appetites' in check, though they are present in his soul because of his lack of education. He holds his evil appetites in check 'not by persuading them that it is better not to act on them or taming them with arguments, but by compulsion and fear, trembling for his other possessions' (*Rep*. VIII 554c). Thus, he is not averse to spending other people's money to satisfy his appetite for luxuries, but he will not contribute his own resources, even for fine ends. Consequently, though his better desires generally control the worse, he is not free from internal civil war, for his 'dronish appetites' for luxury are reined in by his thrift, not by a conviction that they shouldn't be satisfied. His son, the democratic man, shares his father's view that it is fine to spend other people's money on luxuries, and so, taking his father's lesson to heart, he helps himself to his father's fortune.

The democratic man is reared in a 'miserly and uneducated way' by an oligarchic father. He is torn between his father's frugal principles and the life of debauchery promised by his friends. When he tastes the honey of the 'drones' – hedonistic idlers – and associates with people who can provide 'every variety of multicoloured pleasure in every sort of way' (*Rep*. VIII 559d), this turns him from an oligarchic to a democratic orientation. At first, he suffers from internal strife between the oligarchic principles inside him and the unnecessary desires nurtured by his new friends: 'sometimes, the democratic party yields to the oligarchic, so that some of the young man's appetites are overcome, others are expelled, a kind of shame arises in his soul, and order is restored' (*Rep.* VIII 560a). However, since the 'citadel of the young man's soul' – his commanding part – is 'empty of knowledge, fine ways of living, and words of truth', his appetitive desires soon grow numerous and strong, and return to occupy the citadel of his soul. The democratic man then returns to the 'lotus eaters' – or idling 'drones' – and lives with them openly. Having persuaded him that measured and orderly expenditure is boorish and mean, the lotus eaters join forces with his many useless desires, and expel the thrifty part of his soul. They 'return insolence, anarchy extravagance, and shamelessness from exile in a blaze of torch-light, wreathing them in garlands and accompanying them with a vast chorus of followers' (*Rep.* VIII 560e). Revaluing all values, they call insolence good breeding, anarchy freedom, extravagance magnificence, and shamelessness courage, inverting the relationship between virtues and vices that the democratic man inherited from his father. The youth who was brought up with necessary desires hence arrives at the liberation and release of useless and unnecessary pleasures.

When the 'great tumult within him' has spent itself, the frenzy of his youth dies down. The democratic man will then put all pleasures on an equal footing, 'surrendering rule over himself to whichever desire comes along, as if it were chosen by lot. When that one is satisfied, he will surrender rule to another, not disdaining any but satisfying them all equally' (*Rep.* VIII 561b). His overarching principle is that all pleasures are equal and must be valued equally – there is no distinction between pleasures belonging to fine and good desires and pleasures belonging to shameful and base desires that could justify pursuing and valuing the former and restraining the latter:

> And so he lives on, yielding day to day to the desire at hand: Sometimes he drinks heavily while listening to the flute; at other times, he drinks only water and is on a diet; sometimes he goes in for physical training; at other times, he is idle and neglects everything; and sometimes he even occupies himself with what he takes to be philosophy. He often engages in politics, leaping up from his seat and saying and doing whatever comes into his mind. If he happens to admire soldiers, he is carried in that direction, if money-makers, in that one. There is neither order nor necessity in his life, but he calls it pleasant, free, and blessedly happy, and he follows it for as long as he lives. (*Rep.* VIII 561c6–d7)

The democrat thus levels all natural distinctions between his necessary and unnecessary desires, treating them all as equally valuable and worthy of being satisfied. As a result, he becomes a complex and 'multi-coloured' man, full of all sorts of characters, with no order or necessity. His enjoyment of the philosophical or political life is short-lived, a mere simulacrum. True philosophers seek to know the good with their entire being, putting themselves in order and structuring the city into a harmonious whole. They don't treat philosophical puzzles as a pastime. To be a philosopher is to subordinate all desires to the desire to know the truth, so that no desires swim against the philosophical current: 'when someone's desires flow towards learning and everything of that sort' he is concerned with the pleasures of the soul 'itself by itself' and will 'abandon those that come from the body – if indeed he is a true philosopher and not merely a counterfeit one' (*Rep.* VI 485d). The democratic man contains a multitude of characters, then, not because he at times has the true character of the politician, and at other times the true character of the philosopher, but because he sometimes engages in activities that mimic the serious commitments of each. He treats philosophical discussion as a pleasant diversion, rather than a way of life.[45]

Each of these three – the timocrat, oligarch, and democrat – are 'mixed types', torn between different conceptions of the fine and noble. They are thus not single-minded in their pursuit of honour, money, and non-necessary pleasures, but rather veer between two commitments (the timocrat, the oligarch) or flit all over the place (the democratic man). In this respect, they all differ from the aristocratic man and the tyrant, who show a firm commitment to a single goal and thus display greater unity of purpose than any of the other characters.[46]

2.5 Lawlessness and the Will to Power

In each case, the disordered non-rational desires of the young men result in a failure to grasp the nature of the good and either a vacillation between different ideals, or a commitment to the wrong ends. This means that reason fails to do its work. The tyrant's pursuit of pleasure is led by the great winged drone in his soul: erotic love, who acts as a leader of the mob, rousing his appetites and promising that they will achieve satisfaction without restraint under its leadership. The drone, as a leader in the soul, represents reason's endorsement of the indiscriminate pursuit of gratification. It unifies and protects the appetites against the restraint of shame and law, and kills off any beliefs or desires that oppose the indiscriminate pursuit of gratification. These appetites 'need many things to satisfy them'

[45] For insightful analyses, see Scott (2000) and Hitz (2010).

[46] Speaking loosely, we might say that, unlike the oligarch and democrat, neither the aristocrat nor the tyrant is akratic or enkratic due to their unity of purpose. In Aristotle's strict sense, the akratic man (1) makes the right decision, but (2) abandons it (3) due to a desire for base or excessive bodily pleasures (4) that most people can resist. The enkratic man also makes the right decision, despite having an appetite for excessive or base bodily pleasure (*EN* VII). Because the enkratic and the akratic have the *right supposition about the good*, and make the right decision, they are not base or vicious. But the democrat and the oligarch certainly have the *wrong* conception of the good, as does the timocrat, though he initially vacillates. Therefore, they are neither akratic nor enkratic in Aristotle's strict sense.

(*Rep.* IX 573d): 'feasts, revelries, luxuries, and girlfriends, and that sort of thing' (*Rep.* IX 573d), making the tyrant needy. At least initially, he pursues the same kind of pleasures that the democratic man goes in for in youth, and that he also enjoys, intermittently, in old age. Plato describes the life of the democratic man as 'neither slavish nor lawless (*oute aneleutheron oute paranomon*)' (*Rep.* IX 572d2). The democrat has a residual sense of shame, and sometimes restricts his appetites for the sake of his health – perhaps he does dry January or commits to not seeing his Corinthian girlfriend for a while, until he gets bored, and seeks new diversions. His son ends up lacking even the most residual sense of shame when *erōs* assumes command of his soul.[47]

There is a tradition in Greek literature of associating tyrants with luxury and debauchery.[48] It is tempting to think that the tyrant's vice is ultimately an extreme form of intemperance (*akolasia*), and that the tyrant's reasons for pursuing increasingly bizarre pleasures is simply the satisfaction that these objects hold out: on this analysis, he really relishes the taste of human blood and the satisfaction of sex with animals, gods, and parents. This would make him bestial rather than unjust. However, Plato insists that the tyrant suffers from the worst form of injustice. His eagerness to act on paranomic desires suggests that it is *breaking the rule* rather than what is *achieved* by breaking the rule that ultimately attracts the tyrant: the tyrant doesn't use political power as a means to the satisfaction of his desires but seeks political power as an expression of his superiority, expressed by his untrammelled pursuit of pleasures that are prohibited by the laws that bind others. He can do whatever he wants with impunity: that's why he is superior to those he rules, the truly simple-minded. The tyrant's pursuit of lawless objects of pleasure is a consequence rather than a cause of his depravity.[49]

---

[47] 'A man who is mad and deranged attempts to rule not just human beings but gods as well, and expects that he will be able to succeed. – He certainly does. – Then a man becomes tyrannical in the precise sense of the term when either his nature or his way of life or both of them together make him drunk, filled with erotic desire, and mad – Absolutely.' (*Rep.* IX 573c). *Erōs* makes you pursue one goal exclusively and obsessively. But as Scott (2000) has shown, *erōs* lacks a distinct object for Plato; instead, it affects the way in which one pursues a goal. In this regard, Scott argues, the tyrant's *erōs* resembles the philosopher's: both have a single-minded and unwavering commitment to their end.

[48] This backdrop to Plato's analysis is discussed intelligently by Arruzza (2019); see also Larivée (2012). For Alcibiades' lawless character, see Thucydides, 6.15.3–4. Plutarch's *Life of Alcibiades* (16) contains observations that mirror Plato's portrait of the tyrannical character, though it would be a mistake to think that Plato is trying to capture any particular historical figure in his portrait of the tyrant.

[49] Arruzza (2019) misses the cause of the tyrant's lawless vice when she claims that '[t]he tyrant is incapable of governing himself, and hence is a slavish figure, because he is driven by his eroticized appetites rather than by the autonomous judgments of his rational part. His relationship to political power is instrumental to the futile attempt to satisfy his insatiable appetites, as ruling others is taken as the ultimate means to unlimited enjoyment. And precisely for this reason, his subjects are turned into his slaves and instruments of enjoyment' (pp. 182–3).

The tyrant thus seeks to have his way. In so doing, he simultaneously defies the normal relations of ruler and ruled, attempting to master his own father and mother in blatant violation of duties of filial piety.[50] Lawlessness manifests in acts that hubristically defy the sacred and social orders. Breaking into people's houses and looting temples shows complete disregard for what is his own and what is someone else's, of what we owe each other and what we owe the gods. As Dominic Scott puts it, lawless desires involve 'transgression of boundaries that would tend to destroy the very possibility of human relationships, family, and society, not just destabilize them (cf. 580a3–4)' (Scott 2000, p. 139): they are, he says 'blind to the sacred as well as to the social, and the tyrant has cut himself off equally from both' (Scott 2000, p. 139).

This is an apt account of lawlessness as Plato describes it. But the drive to lawlessness is not just a by-product of the tyrant's erotic and single-minded pursuit of pleasure. He does not, it seems, commit acts of incest, cannibalism, murder, and bestiality because such acts help him satisfy his non-necessary desires (it's in any case hard to see how bestiality could be instrumental in this way). Nor does he necessarily derive great pleasure from sleeping with his own mother (however lovely, mum is presumably past her prime). The point of these acts is not (simply) enjoyment of the object of appetite, but the transgression of law itself. Such acts express the tyrant's complete defiance of any authority, whether in the form of human or divine laws. He can tolerate no master, and so he cannot be subject to the same laws that bind the citizens together in a political community or the laws that govern the relations between father and son or man and god. His defiance of such laws – and the fact that he gets away with it – is what establishes his dominance, and this defiance is expressed through his complete freedom from any bonds, even the very bonds that make a community possible. The tyrant is therefore *defined* by his pursuit of lawless pleasures. They express his most deep-seated convictions and his self-conception as a man who is subject to none and master of all. We thus see how the pleonectic drive that Glaucon posited as the natural inclination of mankind in book II leads us to lawlessness when reason and a sense of shame have been entirely removed. The erotic love that the drones implant unleashes forces that were already present in our souls. It gives birth to madness, and this madness is a kind of *hubris*: wanting to rule over the gods, and recognizing no limit to one's power.

It would therefore be a mistake to attempt to shame the tyrant by exposing his behaviour for what it is. The tyrant asserts his dominance precisely by acting in

[50] This failure to honour his superiors is a kind of *hubris* that Socrates decries in the *Apology*. Indeed, the only thing Socrates ever claims to know is that 'it is wicked and shameful to do wrong, to disobey one's superior, be he god or man' (*Apology* 29b).

defiance of moral and legal norms, and when he is called out for his bad behaviour, he simply bares his teeth. He dominates the weak through lawbreaking that acts as a kind of 'vice-signalling'. If justice is 'high-minded simplicity', as Thrasymachus says, and injustice more masterly than justice, then breaking the law is nothing to be ashamed of – provided that you can get away with it. On the contrary, violating norms is valuable along multiple dimensions: in addition to instrumental value, flagrant lawbreaking deters those who consider opposing you and signals to the weak that you are above the law. Power – not satisfaction of desires – is the fundamental motive behind the tyrant's vice. In violating the laws – and so in acting lawlessly – he reveals his true nature.[51]

2.6 "Naturall Equalitie": A Charm?

The tyrant's lawlessness is not a coincidental consequence of his ruthless pursuit of pleasure and luxury, but rather the way in which he asserts his power and unwillingness to be bound by normal laws and conventions. The tyrant is thus opposed to the rule of law, at least as these laws apply to him: he places himself above the law. By committing 'the whole of injustice' and installing himself as a ruler with unlimited powers, he demonstrates that he is by nature entitled to the greatest share of divisible goods in the city.

For the tyrant, fair distribution is relative to worth, but he measures worth in power, expressed through superior stealth and force. His stealth is displayed in acts of dissimulation, when he presents himself as the champion of the poor, as well as in the ruthless plots by which he dispatches his enemies. His force is displayed in acts of gruesome violence that will deter any potential enemy from challenging his rule. While acts of murder and savagery may be instrumental on some occasions, and while the tyrant may choose them as a means to an end, they also assert his status as above the law.

Richard Kraut captures the tyrant's injustice in a note that has reference to Aristotle's account of injustice in the narrow sense, but that seems equally applicable to the mindset of the tyrannical soul in Plato's *Republic*. The pleonectic man's pleasure in lawbreaking derives from his 'general contemptuousness toward the law and those who respect the law' (Kraut 2002, pp. 138–9): '[s]omeone who is unjust in the narrow sense does not regard the suffering of others as a cost [of doing unjust acts], but as part of the appeal of acting unjustly' (p. 139).[52] The tyrant is the quintessentially unjust person, someone who is not

[51] Contrast this with Arruzza (2019, p. 186). For Arruzza, lawlessness is a coincidental consequence of the tyrant's ruthless pursuit of pleasure and luxury.

[52] Kraut (2002) thinks the feeling of *epichairekakia* (spite) is characteristic of the unjust man: he takes pleasure in the (ill-deserved) bad fortune of others (p. 139). If it is deserved, the feeling is righteous indignation (*nemesis*). Since the unjust man, by definition, causes others to suffer

simply soft or self-indulgent, but who treats his share of benefits as a measure of his worth. The ethical outlook of the tyrant – whether in word or in deed – is succinctly summed up by Callicles when he contrasts what is just by nature with what is just by law in the *Gorgias*. It is just by nature, he claims, that the superior should both rule over and have a greater share than his inferiors:

> We mold the best and the most powerful among us, taking them while they are still young, like lion cubs, and with charms and incantations we subdue them into slavery, telling them that one is supposed to get no more than his fair share, and that's what's admirable and just. But surely, if a man who is equal to it arises, he will shake off, tear apart, and escape all of this, he will trample underfoot our documents, our tricks and charms, and all out laws that violate nature. He, the slave, will rise up and be revealed as our master, and here the justice of nature will shine forth (*exelampsen to tēs phuseōs dikaion*). (*Gorg*. 483e–484b)[53]

Contrast this with Hobbes' conception of natural law in the *Leviathan*. Hobbes argues that natural law commands the acknowledgement of 'naturall equalitie', and so recommends the making of peace among equals:

> If in this case, at the making of Peace, men require for themselves, that which they would not have to be granted to others, they do contrary to the precedent law, that commandeth the acknowledgement of naturall equalitie, and therefore also against the law of Nature. The observers of this law, are those we call Modest, and the breakers Arrogant Men. The Greeks call the violation of this law *πλεονεξία*; that is, a desire of more than their share. (Hobbes 1996, pp. 107–8; ch. XV 'of Other Lawes of Nature')

This, in effect, is the conventional conception of justice defended by Glaucon in *Republic* book II. If Thrasymachus is right, it is an inherently unstable agreement, since the assumption of natural equality is false, making democracy naturally prone to a descent into tyranny. On this point, at least, he and Plato agree.

2.7 The Tyrant's Regrets

I started my discussion by observing the paradoxes of tyranny. The tyrannical man is full of disorder and regret, slavery and unfreedom; he is in the greatest need of most things and truly poor; he is 'inevitably envious, untrustworthy,

misfortune unfairly, it is inevitable that his joy will be spiteful (cf. *EN* II.7 1108b2–7; *EE* III.7 1233b16–26). Kenny renders *epichairekakia* as 'malice', which captures the tyrant's outlook.

53 Aristotle's use of the phrase *dialampei to kalon* ('the fine shines through') in discussing the case of King Priam in *EN* I.10 (1100b31) inverts Callicles' use of the verb in the *Gorgias*. For Callicles, what is just by nature shines forth when the slave tramples law underfoot and assumes political power; for Aristotle, the fine shines through when we bear the loss of political power with magnanimity, preserving virtue.

unjust, friendless, impious, host and nurse to every kind of vice, and ... his ruling makes him even more so. And because of all of these, he is extremely unfortunate and goes on to make those near him like himself' (*Rep*. IX 580a). The list of characteristics drives home the tyrant's wretched predicament. But why should we think that Plato is right to attribute these characteristics to the tyrant? After all, he seems to be capable of securing the objects of his appetite, however bizarre, and while he may be poor in spirit, he surely makes up for it in wealth. Why, then, is the tyrant full of regret (*metameleia*)?[54] And though he may make enemies easily, and cannot trust that his allies are friends rather than sycophants, it seems odd to claim that the tyrant is necessarily friendless: he is certainly capable of entertaining a crowd.

These startling claims are easier to understand when we see the tyrant's true objective, namely, to outdo others. Friendship requires reciprocity and equality, two values the tyrant is loath to recognize. He can only succeed if someone else fails, for what he wants is supremacy as a private individual, and what he promotes is his own private interest at the expense of others, which he sees as in competition with the interests of everyone else. By contrast, philosopher rulers are also supreme, but they rule for the sake of the common good, and precisely because they don't aim to advance their own private interests, they can share a common purpose and hence be friends. Thus, even if the tyrant could overcome his paranoid suspicions, and even if his companions could overcome their fear of sudden death, it is structurally impossible for the tyrant to have friends, since that requires seeking the same good as another.

The tyrant's regret also reflects the internal logic of his desire. It is impossible for the tyrant to attain what he wants because he can never achieve happiness by pursuing ends that are inimical to human well-being. His false conception of the good means that he will never get what he wants.[55] His pursuit of increasingly intense and varied pleasures will not result in maximization, for the pleasures slip though his fingers as his mind adapts and falls back into neutrality or pain where

[54] Warren (2022) discusses the sources of the tyrant's regret (pp. 35–83). He finds it puzzling that the tyrannical soul should be 'full of regret'. His puzzlement stems from his assumption that the tyrant's regret is *moral* regret (see p. 55). Warren imagines that in all cases of regret, the agent 'looks back and is pained at the thought that he performed that deed': the agent must 'take responsibility in some sense for the deed in addition to then engaging in self-chastisement with respect to that deed' (p. 55). 'Taking responsibility' and 'chastising oneself' here involves acknowledging and being pained that one acted contrary to the demands of virtue. By contrast, I don't see that either Plato or Aristotle restrict *metameleia* to moral regret (remorse or repentance). While *metameleia* always involves 'a painful retrospective negative assessment of one's own act', as Warren puts it (p. 55), this negative assessment needn't involve an acknowledgement that the act was unjust, cowardly, and so on. Regret can be prudential regret ('I wish I had been cleverer!') or a form of self-pity ('I wish I didn't have to suffer the consequences of my acts!') or shame relative to one's own mistaken ideals ('I'm a real man ... this is beneath my dignity').

[55] For discussion, see Penner (1991).

once there was pleasure. The tyrant regrets his actions, not because he thinks they are morally wrong – he does not – but because they never bring him the satisfaction he craves and, furthermore, have unintended consequences that come back to haunt him: he cannot trust anyone, and lives in fear. That's why he is truly poor and envious. It is not just because his soul is disordered, then, that the tyrant is wretched: the nature of his disease becomes clear when we consider the self-defeating internal logic of unleashing the swarm of desires locked up in the human soul.

3 Vice and Moral Ignorance in the *Nicomachean Ethics*

3.1 Justice and the Common Good

Plato assumes that talents are unequally distributed: only a minority of citizens are naturally equipped to be educated in statecraft. In the *Politics*, Aristotle concedes that if naturally superior rulers existed among humans, then it would be just for them to rule. Demanding that a man pre-eminent in virtue should be ruled in turn would be as if mankind should claim to rule over Zeus, dividing up his offices: 'the only alternative is that all should happily obey such a ruler, according to what seems to be the order of nature, and that men like him should be kings in their states for life' (*Pol.* III 13 1284b30–4).[56]

Aristotle holds that absolute kingship, where a pre-eminent person or group of people govern with a view to the common good, is the best form of rule. Tyranny is a corruption of kingship: one man rules over the others like a master over slaves. He rules in his own interest rather than for the common good. But although absolute kingship is the best form of government in the abstract, divine men are not often found. When we consider the matter empirically, we will find that citizens tend to be roughly equal in their capacity for holding public office and discharging the role of ruler well. The best form of government for most communities is a polity (*politeia*), where citizens conduct political life for the common good. The corrupt form of a polity is democracy in the pejorative sense: rule by the dispossessed masses rather than rule by decent citizens who own households and who take turns to hold public offices. Aristotle therefore accepts the reality of what Hobbes calls a '*naturall equalitie*' between citizens, not just because the weak can unite against the strong, as Hobbes observes, but more

[56] Aristotle's claim raises a series of questions, given his definition of the citizen in a strict sense (*Pol.* III 13 1283b42–84a1). The absolute king seems to be both a citizen and not a citizen. Absolute kingship is intelligently discussed by Lockwood (2020). Aristotle maintains that if the gap in virtue and political abilities is too wide, there is no justice between superior and inferior, and hence no political community. For those pre-eminent in virtue, there is no law – they are themselves a law (*Pol.* III 13 1284a13). Anyone who attempted to make laws for them would be ridiculous: they would receive the same retort as the lions gave to the hares in Antisthenes' story of the council of the animals 'when the hares began haranguing the lions and claiming equality for all' (*Pol.* III 13 1284a15–18).

fundamentally because *individual* citizens are roughly equal in their capacity for deliberative and judicial wisdom. Justice is each citizen receiving honours proportionate to his worth, and their worth is roughly equal. Aristotle observes that we learn how to rule by first occupying the position of subject, and later assuming the role of ruler, just as a general first needs to learn how to take orders from his superior as a soldier before he develops the expertise required to lead.[57] The best constitution for most cities, then, is polity, not absolute kingship.[58]

This position informs Aristotle's approach to virtue and vice: Aristotle's *Ethics* describes the perfections needed to be a good citizen. A citizen is one who shares in ruling and being ruled (*Pol.* III 13 1283b42–84a1) and, in the best state, citizens decide to rule and be ruled with a view to the life of virtue. Conversely, if we want to know what states of character undermine the pursuit of the common good, we should consider what character traits make us worse as citizens taking part in all aspects of public life, and taking turns at ruling and being ruled – that is, who do not always hold public office, but remain subject to the decisions of courts and assemblies.

3.2 Injustice, Strife and Enmity

Justice in general, claims Aristotle, is the whole of virtue, while conversely, injustice in general is the whole of vice (*EN* V.1 1130a10–11). This type of justice is 'complete virtue in relation to another' (*EN* V.1 1129b27–30). General justice is equivalent to lawfulness, while injustice is lawlessness. The law 'prescribes living in accord with each virtue, and forbids living in accord with each vice' (*EN* V.2 23–5). As a result, most lawful actions are produced by virtue as a whole, rather than by the special virtue concerned with the distribution of honours or wealth or safety or any other benefit or burden that can be divided among members of a political community who share in a political system. This type of distribution is the domain of special justice and injustice, which concerns how we relate to another's good in matters of distribution and rectification of benefits and harms.

Justice keeps communities together, and it extends as far as friendship (*philia*) between the citizens. Injustice, conversely, causes strife and enmity, and undermines the cohesion and happiness of the state.[59] In pursuing their

[57] The good citizen should 'know how to govern like a free man, and obey like a free man, and these are the virtues of a citizen' (*Pol.* III 4 1277b15–16). While it is only *qua* ruler that the citizen possesses practical wisdom (*phronēsis*) in public affairs, the ruled possess it coincidentally (a person in possession of the medical art would be able to heal themselves *qua* doctor, but not *qua* patient).

[58] See Schofield (2011).

[59] Aristotle agrees with Plato that injustice 'causes civil war, hatred and fighting' among the citizens, while justice brings 'friendship (*philia*) and a sense of common purpose (*homonoia*)' (*Rep.* I 351d).

private interests, unjust citizens inadvertently compromise their own happiness. The political community is naturally prior to the households and individuals that make it up, claims Aristotle: parts derive their function from the whole that they subserve. Just as the function of organic parts like hands and feet is relative to the activity of the whole organic body, the function of households and individuals is relative to the activity of the city. Its purpose is self-sufficiency and eudaimonia for the community and its constituent parts: citizens and the households that they lead. An individual separated from a city may live, unlike severed hands and feet, but he will not live well. The Cyclops in his cave, 'laying down the rules for his children and wife' (*Odyssey* 9.114, quoted by Aristotle in *EN* X.9 1180a29 and Plato in *Laws* 680b–c) leads a pre-political life, and cannot be happy, even if he has a rich provision of external goods. Everyone, claims Aristotle, has a natural impulse towards political community. Those who are self-sufficient, or incapable of political community, are either beasts or gods: 'For this is distinctive of human beings in contrast to the other animals, that they are the only ones with a perception of good and bad, and just and unjust, and so on; and it is community in these that produces a household and a city' (*Pol.* I.2 1253a15–18, trans. modified from Irwin and Fine).

Human self-sufficiency is only achieved in the city, because it is the realisation of a specifically human life form: the political. Like Plato, Aristotle maintains that justice causes human community while injustice promotes enmity; that is why good laws are required for a community to prosper. Justice is an efficient cause of eudaimonia (without justice, no community will flourish) and a quality of the interactions that make up the shared life of virtuous citizens, and hence their happiness. The capacity for virtue and vice of character is distinctly human. While virtue 'completes' and perfects human nature, vice corrupts and destroys it. This makes human nature Janus-faced: we occupy the extremes of the continuum between best and worst in the animal world: 'Just as a human being is the best of the animals if he has been completed, he is also the worst of them if he is separated from law and the rule of justice' (*Pol.* I.2 1253a31–3).

The reason, claims Aristotle, is that

> injustice is most formidable when it is armed, and a human being naturally grows up armed and equipped for intelligence and virtue but can most readily use this equipment for ends that are contrary to intelligence and virtue; hence, without virtue he is the most unscrupulous and savage of animals, the most excessive in the pursuit of sex and food. Justice, however, is political: for the rule of justice is an order in the political community. (*Pol.* I.2 31–6).

Justice guards against the bad effects of injustice, and it does this best when it is enshrined in law and absorbed in the characters of the citizens.

In seeking the vices that corrupt the constitution and the city, Aristotle thinks we should not focus on the vices of the tyrant, which belong in the realm of psychopathology, but rather the human vices that afflict the citizens in a state that is suited for constitutional democracy. These vices, which are states with regard to natural and necessary pleasures and pains, prevent citizens from working towards the common good. Desires that are neither natural nor necessary are the domain of bestial vice and bestial *akrasia* (*EN* VII.5), which need to be studied as the pathological states they are, alongside other diseased states, such as madness.[60] In keeping with his analysis in the *Nicomachean Ethics*, in the *Politics* Aristotle defines this common good as a life of activity in accord with virtue that encompasses all the citizens who have freedom to take part in public affairs. The *Politics* does not itself identify these vices or discuss them at length, except obliquely, though Aristotle discusses flawed constitutions at length.[61] Aristotle does, however, make frequent reference to his *Ethics* throughout the *Politics*, and so we can supplement his analysis with the analysis of character in the ethical works. In a polity, the good person and the good citizen will coincide, claims Aristotle, at least to the extent that citizens are equipped both to be ruled and to rule.[62] Conversely, a bad citizen will lack these virtues, and may even acquire outright vices, states that are inimical to the pursuit of the common good. Since the citizen can only realize his individual happiness as part of a state, states of character that impede the realization of the common good will also harm the citizens' own interests, and make their lives less blessed and happy.

3.3 Virtue, Vice and Function

For Aristotle, as for Plato, human virtue and vice are forms of natural goodness and natural badness.[63] Aristotle inherits Plato's view of virtue and vice as relative to function, and hence to kind. The virtue of x is the state (*hexis*) of x which causes it to function *well* as a thing of its kind, while the vice of x is the

60 'One sort of vice is human, and this is called simple vice (*hē men kat' anthrōpon haplōs legetai mocthēria*); another sort is called vice with an added condition (*hē de kata prosthesin*) and is said to be bestial (*thēriōdēs*) or diseased (*nosēmatōdēs*) vice, but not simple vice (*haplōs d'ou*). Similarly, it is clear that one sort of *akrasia* is bestial, another diseased, but only the *akrasia* corresponding to human intemperance is simple *akrasia* (*haplōs de hē kata anthrōpinēn akolasian monē*)' (*EN* VII.5 1149a16–20).

61 Aristotle further criticizes Socrates for his account of the revolutions from one constitution to another in *Pol.* 5.12 131540ff.

62 They coincide, since the polis perfects human nature. We come into our own as human beings when we are citizens in a polis.

63 For a defence of Aristotle's version of this analysis, see Foot (2001).

state of x which causes it to function *badly* as a thing of its kind.[64] Living things are defined by their capacity for growth, locomotion, perception, and so on. These are powers the living thing has in virtue of being ensouled. The virtue of a *living* thing is whatever psychological state enables it to be active in the best way as the kind of being it is; its vice whatever psychological state prevents it from being active in the best way for a thing of its kind. At the most general level, then, virtue and vice, and hence goodness and badness, can be defined as the same for all living creatures. But what it is to be a good or bad bee, horse or human will differ according to the life form that is characteristic of different species (see e.g. *EN* II.6 1106a19).

Pinning down the exact nature of human vice as Aristotle understands it is more challenging than analysing Plato's conception of vice. Plato tackles vice head-on in books VIII–IX of the *Republic*. Aristotle only discusses vice obliquely. For Plato, vice is any falling away from perfected reason that results in false beliefs about the good, and so any deviation from the good order that characterizes justice.[65] Aristotle denies that any character trait that makes us act contrary to correct reason or experience conflict between reason and passion should automatically be classified as a vice. Vice should not be confused with *akrasia* – lapses caused by strong non-rational desires that most humans share. The simple akratic retains the right principle when his mind is not clouded by passion, and this means he is not vicious. Nor is vice due to lawless desires, as in the most frightening cases of bestiality. While madness, disease, or habit can cause horrific actions, caused by desires that aren't natural or necessary for a human, they are not the main concern of political science.[66]

---

64 See the function argument in *Rep.* I 352e–354a. Aristotle develops his own version of the function argument in *EN* I.7, concluding that happiness is activity of the soul in accord with virtue. He does not draw any inferences about immortality, however.

65 Plato argues that good order is preserved in the souls of lawful subjects, even if they do not themselves grasp the nature of the good, provided that they retain true beliefs about the good. True beliefs about the good are preserved when spirit and appetite are subservient to reason – whether in another (the wise ruler) or by laws that embody reason. If subjects don't rebel, but acquiesce in the rule of reason, they will possess the virtues appropriate for subjects, though they lack temperance, courage, wisdom, and justice.

66 Although Aristotle appears to classify *akrasia* as a vice (*mochthēria*) at *EE* II.7 1223a36–7 and 1223b30–2, these passages report how things have seemed (*hē d'akrasia mochthēria dokei einai; hē d'akrasia mochthēria tis phainetai*; cf. *EN* VII.1 1145b9ff.). Not all states that fall short of virtue are vices. In *EN* VII.8, Aristotle contrasts virtue (*aretē*) and vice (*mochthēria*), and argues that virtue preserves the principle of action, while vice destroys it. A few lines on, he contrasts the continent person's state, calling it excellent (*spoudaios*) compared to the incontinent person's state, which he calls base (*phaulos*). This has been taken to suggest that Aristotle is prepared to treat a non-vicious state (*akrasia*) as base, and a non-virtuous state (*enkrateia*) as excellent, which is striking on its face, since he elsewhere denies that *enkrateia* is a form of virtue and *akrasia* a form of vice (e.g. *EN* VII.8 1151a5ff.). Perhaps what he has in mind is that the enkratic person's state is good *insofar as* he retains a good principle (though it is not good

Drawing on ancient medical theory, Aristotle defines virtue as a state that makes us 'hit the mean' in action and feeling. The mean – *to meson* – is what is appropriate given the particulars of our situation. Each virtue has its own domain of action and feeling. Generosity concerns the use of wealth: the generous person gives to the right people, at the right time, taking wealth from the right sources and isn't pained by parting with his money. The courageous person has the right feeling of fear and confidence in the context of war, and acts accordingly. Virtues are states that are intermediate because they make us hit the mean in action and feeling. Each is flanked by a state of excess and deficiency. The coward and the rash person both fail to hit the mean, the coward because he is too fearful or lacks sufficient confidence, while the rash person tends to be overconfident, and insufficiently fearful. The wasteful person and the ungenerous person likewise fail to hit the mean, by acquiring and disbursing their wealth in ways that are deficient or excessive relative to the standards observed by the generous person. For Aristotle, then, there are, with a few notable exceptions, two bad states flanking each virtue, a vice of deficiency and a vice of excess. The magnanimous person has the right attitude to honours, while the pusillanimous and vain man fail in opposite ways. The mild man has the right attitude to anger, while the irascible and the 'inirascible' persons do not. The boor and the buffoon fail where the witty person succeeds; the quarrelsome and ill-tempered person fails at friendliness, but so do the ingratiating person and the flatterer.

The catalogue of virtues and vices contains the character states that promote friendship and common purpose for a political community, and those that cause enmity and strife. Most fundamentally, vices are states of character that all make us bad at doing what virtue does well in their respective domains, though this specification still needs to be made more precise to be informative.

Importantly, Aristotle denies that I need a generous disposition to do a generous act, or a cowardly disposition to do a cowardly act, and so on. We can do these acts coincidentally, without having the purpose that the person with the corresponding character trait possesses. The stingy person is pained by parting with his money even when it's appropriate to contribute to a cause; he shirks his duties because he thinks it is *right* that he should hold on to his money, even at the expense of the well-being of his friends and family. We can also

without qualification), while the akratic's is base, insofar as he abandons his decision (but not therefore base without qualification). We don't make sense of Aristotle's remarks by focusing only on the idea that *phaulos* here covers ordinary, run-of-the-mill akratics, unlike the *mochthēroi*. For in that case, we would have to explain why Aristotle also includes continents among people whose character is *excellent*, contrary to his general view. Furthermore, the incontinent agent is only base in a way, since the akratic is similar to the intemperate insofar as he does the same act (*EN* VII.8 1151a5–9), though his state differs. For the intemperate agent decides on the intemperate act, while the akratic does not.

perform an act that is stingy without realizing it (not understanding that the person in front of us has a real need), in which case our stingy act is involuntary, and not blameworthy. Only non-culpable ignorance of particular facts makes acts involuntary, and so exempt from praise and blame, however. If we are ignorant of normative facts – which acts are good and which acts are bad, which acts are in accord with the virtues and which are not – our ignorance is always culpable, since it amounts to ignorance about the good.[67]

I believe we come closer to an understanding of Aristotle's general account of vice if we start from his claim in *Nicomachean Ethics* book II that virtues are 'decisions of some kind, or rather require decision' (*prohaireseis tines ē ouk aneu prohaireseōs*) (*EN* II.5 1106a4–5). Aristotle defines virtue as a 'state that decides (*hexis prohairetikē*), consisting in a mean, the mean relative to us, which is defined by reference to reason' (*EN* II.6 1107a1–3). It is a state that decides, since it deliberates with a view to an end, and its decisions hit the mean in action and feeling because it grasps both which ends are good and how those ends should be pursued in action, and desires them accordingly. This makes virtue a state that unites correct reason with correct desire. Aristotle distinguishes states that are merely emotional and behavioural dispositions – tendencies to experience feelings and to act in certain ways – from states that reveal the agent's conception of the good, expressed in his *prohairesis*. That is why he demands that feelings reflect the agent's decision to express his state of character. As he puts it in *EN* II.5, 'neither virtues nor vices are feelings'. We are praised or blamed, not for *having* feelings, but rather if we are well or badly off with regard to feelings:

> for we do not praise the angry or frightened person, and do not blame the person who is simply angry, but only the person who is angry in a particular way. We are praised or blamed, however, insofar as we have virtues or vices. Further, we are angry or afraid without decision; but the virtues are decisions of some kind or rather require decision. (*EN* II.5 1105b33–6a5)

In the *Eudemian Ethics*, Aristotle makes explicit what we can infer from his analysis of virtue in the *EN*, namely, that the vices, too, are states that decide, for there are some ways of hitting the mean with respect to emotions that fall short of being virtuous, and similarly some ways of failing to hit the mean that fall short of vice: 'Though all these mean points are praiseworthy, they are not virtues, nor are their opposites vices, since they do not involve decision (*prohairesis*)' (*EE* III.7 1234a24–5).

[67] There is no way to describe virtuous activity without using morally imbued terms: the generous person gives at the right time, to the right people, in the right way, taking wealth from the right sources; he is not simply someone inclined to give freely.

Just as virtue is defined as a '*hexis prohairetikē*' – a state that decides on actions that are in the mean, and so correct (*EN* II.6, 1107a1–3) – vice is also a state that makes decisions but, in this case, a state that decides on actions that deviate from the virtuous mean because the agent has the wrong conception of what is good. This entails that any account of Aristotle's theory of vice that makes the vicious agent a mere 'mass of conflicts' (as Annas (1993 p. 554) puts it; see also Annas (1977)), or 'unprincipled' in the sense that he lacks an overarching *prohairesis*, articulating his notion of the good and his deliberative belief about how to promote it (Müller 2015), will fail to meet criteria that Aristotle explicitly endorses in his ethical works. The agent's *prohairesis* encapsulates his choice of end (articulated in his practical wish) as well as the actions that he thinks should be done for the sake of this end (see Nielsen 2022). Insofar as the *archē* of the vicious agent in 'corrupted' (*EN* VII.8 1151a15; VI.5 1140b19–20: *estin gar hē kakia phthartikē archēs*), he does not pursue the good, which is the object of *boulēsis*, simply speaking (*haplōs*, *EN* III.4, 1113a23–7). Instead, the vicious person pursues things that strike him as good, but that aren't. His principle (*archē*) is corrupted, then, *not* insofar as he lacks a principle altogether, and is entirely unprincipled (as Müller has urged), but, instead, insofar as habituation has perverted his natural end.[68] For Aristotle, a false conception of the good is the result of deficient or wrong habituation – if we are not corrupted, then we will pursue our own good by nature.[69]

This also explains why Aristotle speaks of ignorance of the good in *Nicomachean Ethics* book III as 'ignorance in the decision' (*hē en tēi prohairesei agnoia*, *EN* III.1 1110b33), for the agent's decision encapsulates his conception of the end, insofar as what is chosen is chosen for its sake, so that if the conception of the end (i.e., what is beneficial) is false, the decision will also in some sense be 'ignorant' of the end that is the natural and proper object of wish – namely, the good itself. Vice makes us miss the target, not because we are mistaken about matters of fact (who is acting, what he is doing, about what or to what he is doing it, what he is doing it with, what the result will be, and how he is doing it, *EN* III.1 1111a3–7), which Aristotle calls the 'particulars' of the act, but rather because the target is itself wrong: we are mistaken about what *end* we should pursue

[68] Müller (2015) allows that the vicious agent can have reasons for acting as they do, typically related to what pleases or pains them most in the moment, but these reasons do not reflect a stable conception around which they organize their lives. By contrast, I take *kakia* to involve a stable disposition, organized around a false conception of what kind of life one should live.

[69] This is also the sense in which the principle is 'preserved' in akratic agents (*EN* VII.8 1151a24–5), who have the right conception of the good, even if they do not reliably act on it. As Aristotle says in *EN* III.4, 'Without qualification, and in reality, what is wished is the good, but for each person what is wished is the apparent good . . . . For the excellent person, then, what is wished will be what is wished in reality, while for the base person what is wished is whatever it turns out to be [that appears good to him]' (1113a23–7). Thus, what is destroyed by vice is the good principle.

(*EN* III.5 1110b28–1111a3). This condition can be described interchangeably as 'ignorance about the universal' and 'ignorance in the decision' (*hē en tēi prohairesei agnoia*). In contrast to Socrates, Aristotle thinks it is blameworthy, since the agent has replaced good ends with bad, and so has allowed himself to be corrupted. As he says, 'Every vicious person is ignorant of the actions he must do and avoid, and this sort of error makes people unjust, and in general bad' (*EN* III.5 1110b29–30). Moral ignorance consists in false beliefs about how one should live.

3.4 Aristotle on Moral Ignorance

We can articulate a fuller conception of vice on Aristotle's behalf by considering his remarks in *EN* III.1–5 in the context of the discussion of virtue of character in *EN* II.4. Aristotle here clarifies his account of virtue and habituation in response to an objection, and highlights what it takes to be a virtuous agent. The objection he considers is this: if doing just actions is what it is to be a just person, then I will already possess justice in virtue of behaving in a certain way, and similarly for vicious acts and the trait of vice. In that case, Aristotle's theory of habituation has no explanatory power, for explanandum and explanans would coincide. Aristotle responds by distinguishing between the character of the act and the state of the agent when he does it:

> For acts in accord with the virtues to be done temperately or justly, it does not suffice that they themselves have the right qualities. Rather, the agent must also be in the right state when he does them. First, he must know [that he is doing virtuous actions]; second, he must decide on them and decide on them for themselves; and third, he must do them from a firm and unchanging state. (*EN* II.4 1105a29–35).

This yields three criteria for acting virtuously:

(1) The *knowledge* criterion (he must know that his acts are virtuous).
(2) The *decision* criterion (he must (i) decide on virtuous acts and (ii) decide on them for themselves).
(3) The *state* criterion (he must do so from a firm and unchanging state).

We are now in position to see that these conditions have counterparts for vicious agents. The vicious agent is vicious since he has a false conception of the end he should be aiming at (*EN* III.I 1110b34). There can be no such thing as 'clear-eyed' vice on Aristotle's score: knowing that one's ends are bad and nevertheless pursuing them. Vicious agents have a false supposition about the end, and this means that even if they hit the target that they have set up for themselves, they miss the mean, since the target is off mark. But if they don't know what end they should be aiming at, then they won't even know that they are vicious, since this presupposes knowing that their supposition about the end is false. As Aristotle notes, 'the vicious person does not recognize that he is vicious, whereas the incontinent person recognizes that he is incontinent' (*EN* VII.8 1150b36–7). Ignorance of the universal therefore entails a failure of self-knowledge.

It follows that Aristotle's distance from Socrates is not great as far as their *diagnosis* of vice is concerned. Where they part ways is in their assessment of its blameworthiness. Whereas Socrates holds that ignorance of good and bad excuses, Aristotle thinks we act voluntarily, and so are proper subjects of praise and blame, as long as we know the relevant particulars. Not knowing the quality of one's own ends and adopting the wrong means as a result is not an excuse, for there are certain truths that we are required to know.[70] Aristotle further maintains that vice requires rational endorsement of ends as good, which as a matter of fact are bad. It is not enough habitually to do acts of intemperance or acts of boastfulness to be intemperate or boastful, for I can habitually do such acts without judging them to be right. In the case of the boaster, Aristotle says, 'It is not a person's capacity, but his decision, that makes him a boaster; for his state of character makes a person a boaster, just as it makes a person a liar' (*EN* VI.7 1127b15–17). This conforms to his remarks about injustice in book V.8, where he distinguishes the person who does unjust acts from the unjust person. When someone inflicts a harm in knowledge of the particulars, but without previous deliberation, as when he acts on appetites and spirited desires that are necessary and natural for a human being, he does an act of injustice, 'but he is not thereby unjust or wicked, since it is not vice that causes him to inflict the harm. But whenever decision is the cause, he is unjust and vicious' (*EN* V.8 1135b1135b20–6). When someone inflicts harm in knowledge of the particulars, and on decision, he is vicious and unjust, whereas when he acts in knowledge of the particulars, but his act is caused by natural appetitive or spirited desires, he does an unjust *act*, but isn't thereby unjust or wicked. This indicates that Aristotle sees a parallel between the criteria for acting virtuously laid out in *EN* II.4, and the criteria for acting viciously, and hence for being vicious, for the vicious agent must decide on vicious acts, and does not simply do them from appetite or spirit.[71]

Do vicious agents also choose vicious acts for their own sakes? They do not, if by this we mean that they choose them because they *know* that they are vicious, and think this makes them attractive. Aristotle's vicious man typically

[70] The laws explain what kinds of acts are praiseworthy and blameworthy, and inform the citizens' education. See Aristotle's remarks at the head of *EN* III.1 and his remarks about good laws at the end of book X.

[71] For further discussion of *EN* II.4, see Hampson (2021), Müller (2018), and Jimenez (2016).

thinks he is hitting the mean, and he accuses the virtuous of missing the target.[72] Instead, Aristotle's vicious agent decides on vicious acts for the sake of the very properties that make the virtuous shun them. As he says in book VII, the intemperate man 'pursues excesses of pleasant things because they are excesses and because he decides on it, for themselves and not for some further result' (*hēi kath'huperbolas kai dia prohairesin, di' autas kai mēden di heteron apobainon akolastos*, *EN* VII.7 1150a19–22, following Mb (=cod. Marcianus) rather than the Oxford Classical Text (OCT)). Aristotle does not mean that he aims at excess as his intentional object, but rather that the very properties that would make a prudent man say the acts are excessive make them attractive to the vicious man.

Finally, Aristotle treats vice, just like virtue, as a 'firm and unchanging state'. In this context, what matters is not whether vice is an unchange*able* state – or literally irreversible – but whether Aristotle ascribes a degree of stability to the vicious man parallel to the stability he attributes to the virtuous. In his discussion of the dissolution of friendship in *EN* IX.3, Aristotle allows the virtuous man to backslide – he asks what we should do when our friend, who was good, has become bad, and answers that we should go to every length to try to restore his character, and only give up the friendship if he becomes incurably base. And in *EN* III.5, Aristotle remarks that the unjust or intemperate agent will not become just or temperate simply by wishing to be so – and by revising their conception of the good informing their wish. Like those who acquire curable bodily vices, a resolution without a change of habits won't alter his character, and making the resolution isn't what is hard. This means that vicious agents can have stable and unchanging characters without being incurably wicked.

It would seem, then, that Aristotle attributes counterparts of the agent-criteria for virtuous activity to vicious activity. The vicious agent does vicious acts in ignorance of their badness; he decides on them, and decides on them for their own sakes (for the reasons because of which they are in fact vicious); and does so from a firm and unchanging state. To be vicious is to have adopted a false view of what is fine and worthy of pursuit, and to act on the basis of this conception.

3.5 Are the Vicious Conflicted?

In the course of discussing friendship and self-love in *EN* IX.4, Aristotle makes a remark that has caused deep puzzlement among readers: vicious agents

[72] Aristotle observes that the intermediate states are excessive in comparison to the deficiencies and deficient in comparison to the excesses: 'For the brave person, for instance, appears rash in comparison to the coward, and the cowardly in comparison to the rash person . . . That is why each of the extreme people tries to push the intermediate person to the other extreme, so that the coward, for instance, calls the brave person rash, and the rash person calls him a coward, and similarly with the other cases' (*EN* II.9 1108b17–27).

(*mochthēroi/phauloi*) have conflicted souls (*stasiadzei gar autōn hē psuchē*, 1166b19) like akratic agents (*hoion hoi akrateis*), and they are also plagued by regrets (*metameleias gemousin* 1166b26). These claims have taken many readers by surprise, for in *EN* VII.7 (1150a19–23; b29; 1151a5–7) Aristotle has argued that *akolasia* is in accordance with decision (*kata prohairesin*), and that consequently the *akolastos* is bound *not* to suffer regrets (*anankē gar touton mē einai metamelētikon*, 1150a22; cf. b30–1). Because the intemperate agent acts in accord with his own decision, he does not discover that he has abandoned his commitment after the act. Consequently, he is not pained by realizing that he has acted contrary to his own commitments and what he considers fine, unlike the the akratic agent. The *akolastos* is therefore said to be incurable (*aniatos*).[73] Are the vicious conflicted, as *EN* IX.4 appears to suggest, or must Aristotle's vicious person be unconflicted to avoid collapsing into the akratic and enkratic agent? Aristotle's taxonomy in book VII appears to be under strain once we reach IX.4.

If we assume that all psychological conflict is a conflict between an agent's decision and his appetites, and that all regret is moral regret, Aristotle's claims in VIII.7 and IX.4 seem flat-out contradictory.[74] Could the incurably wicked *akolastos* in IX.4 be a different kind of *mochthēros* and *phaulos* than the bad man (*kakos*) we encounter in VII.7? If the puzzling remarks in IX.4 concern moderately base people, like hoi polloi, the contradiction would seem to disappear, at least if we allow that Aristotle classifies akratics as *mochthēroi* and *phauloi*. Scholars like Grant, Stewart, Gauthier and Jolif, Barney, and Warren have therefore proposed that Aristotle is speaking of a series of different people in IX.4, so that the same terms are used to pick out characters with very different profiles in the course of one paragraph. On this interpretation, instead of taking over Plato's view of the vicious man as conflicted and plagued by

[73] The claim that the *akolastos* is incurable rests on the name and the connection with *koladzein*, to discipline. Elsewhere (e.g. *EN* III.5), Aristotle draws a distinction between curable and incurable vice. Presumably, then, not all forms of intemperance are incurable.

[74] Gauthier and Jolif (1970) in their note ad IX 4 1166b6–7 agree with Grant (1866) that Aristotle is guilty of a contradiction: he sets out to portray the vicious, but instead describes the akratic. The reason is that he is carried away by 'un excès de zèle: dans son désir de refuser au vicieux la bénefice de la bonne conscience, il lui a appliqué illégitimement des conclusions établies pour d'autres que pour lui' ['an excess of zeal: in his desire to deny the vicious the benefit of a good conscience, he illegitimately applied to him conclusions established for others than for him']. Annas (1977) likewise concludes that Aristotle's account is inconsistent, hypothesizing that he did not get around to revising it. Broadie (1991, p. 177, n. 44) replies to Annas. Harmonizing views are defended in Irwin (2001), Brickhouse (2003), Broadie and Rowe (2002, pp. 419–20), and Grönroos (2015). Müller (2015) has argued that Aristotle's account of vice is consistent, but not in the way traditionally supposed: the vicious man is unprincipled. Barney (2020) wishes to sidestep the debate, but thinks the analyses of Grant (1866), Stewart (1892), and Gauthier and Jolif (1971) show that IX.4 is not about vice after all.

regrets, the 'Platonizing' tendency of IX.4 is a mere appearance despite the apparent allusions to Plato's portrait of the tyrant in the passage.[75]

The image of the vicious man as principled remains constant throughout the *Nicomachean Ethics* (III.11 1119a1–6; VII.7 1150a19–22; IX.4 1166b7–10). Indeed, it is needed for Aristotle's taxonomy.[76] In book VII, Aristotle classifies virtuous, encratic, akratic, and vicious agents according to the quality of their decisions (*prohairesis*) and the degree to which their non-rational desires reject the actions that reason enjoins them to do. The virtuous agent makes the right decision and stands by it. He does not have excessive or base desires for sensuous pleasure. There is no element in him 'clashing and struggling with reason' (*machetai kai antiteinei tōi logōi*) (*EN* I.13, 1102b17–18). The enkratic makes the right decision and abides by it, despite having excessive or base appetites, and so he suffers from a conflict of desire before he acts, but reason holds sway. The akratic makes the right decision, but abandons it due to appetite. When he realizes what he has done, he regrets the act because he knows that it is contrary to the demands of virtue, which he recognizes and values. Like the virtuous agent, the vicious agent acts in accordance with his decision and does not regret his act (see also *EN* I.13 1102bff. and III.2 1111b14–19), and so one might infer that he is his own friend.

It is this taxonomy that comes under pressure in IX.4, and that has led some critics, like Grant, Gauthier and Jolif, and Annas to claim that Aristotle would be contradicting himself if he meant to speak of the vicious.[77] In IX.4, Aristotle describes base people (*hoi phauloi*) as at the mercy of their appetites, though here, unlike in VII, he claims that they experience internal conflict. For base people:

> are at odds with themselves (*diapherontai heautois*) and have an appetite for one thing (*heterōn men epithumousin*) and a wish for another (*alla de boulontai*), as incontinent people do (*hoion hoi akrateis*). For they do not choose things that seem to be good for them, but instead choose pleasant things that are actually harmful (*hairountai gar anti tōn dokountōn heautois agathōn einai ta hēdea blabera onta*); and cowardice and laziness causes others to shrink from doing what they think is best for themselves (*ha oiontai beltista einai*). And those who have done many terrible actions hate and shun life because of their vice (*dia tēn mochthērian*), and destroy themselves

[75] Several critics have commented on the Platonizing tendency in Aristotle's discussion in IX.4: for example, Dirlmeier (1960, p. 546, n. 5); Broadie and Rowe (2002, ad 1166b5–7, p. 419).

[76] Aristotle's refusal to call a state *a vice* unless it is a *hexis prohairetikē* (*EE* II. 7 1234a24–5) is retained in his treatment of particular virtues and vices in the *Nicomachean Ethics*.

[77] Annas conjectures that IX.4 belongs to an earlier phase of Aristotle's thought where he aimed to respond to puzzles about friendship from Plato's *Lysis*. The (alleged) incoherence between VII and IX.4 thus reflects Aristotle's 'preference for local rather than global systematization' (Annas (1977, p. 554).

> (*anhairounsin heautous*).[78] Besides, vicious people (*mochthēroi)* seek others to pass their days with, and shun themselves. For when they are by themselves they remember many disagreeable actions (*pollōn kai duschērōn*), and anticipate others in the future; but they manage to forget these in other people's company. These people have nothing lovable about them and so have no friendly feelings for themselves. Hence such a person does not share his own enjoyments and distresses. For his soul is in conflict (*stasiadzei gar autōn hē psuchē*), and because he is vicious (*dia mochthērian*) one part is distressed at being restrained, and another is pleased [by the intended action]; and so each part pulls (*helkei*) in a different direction, as though they were tearing him apart. Even if he cannot be distressed and pleased at the same time, still he is soon distressed because he was pleased, and wishes these things had not become pleasant to him; for base people are full of regrets. (*EN* IX.4 1166b7–25)

Aristotle's depiction of the vicious as internally divided and 'not sharing his own enjoyments and distresses', and as 'having a desire for one thing and a wish for another, as incontinent people do' initially seems to directly contradict the description of the *akolastos* from book VII.[79] Gauthier and Jolif therefore propose that the passage cited concerns those who are akratic, and therefore bad (*phauloi*), rather than the vicious.[80] Only in the final lines ('and those who have done many terrible actions . . . ') does he return to the truly vicious that were the pretext for the analysis in line b5. There are many reasons to resists this attempt at reconciliation, however. The proposal makes it puzzling why Aristotle should *compare* moderately bad people to akratics, if they really *are* akratics.[81] Furthermore, there are many types of psychological conflict.

[78] A euphemism for suicide, as Warren (2022, p. 102, n. 8) notes.

[79] The *akolastos* 'pursues excesses of pleasant things because they are excesses and because he decides on it, for themselves and not for some further result' (*hēi kath'huperbolas kai dia prohairesin, di' autas kai mēden di heteron apobainon akolastos*) (*EN* VII.7 1150a19–22, following Mb (=cod. Marcianus) rather than the OCT).

[80] Gauthier and Jolif (1970), commentary ad 1166b6–7, take the referent of *phauloi* to change back and forth in the lead-up to the argument at b3–7. Commenting on *phaulois* at b6–7, they state: 'Le mot de *phauloi* "mauvaises gens" désigne ici les incontinents dont Aristote va faire le portrait, alors que trois lignes plus haut, 1166b3, le mēme mot de *phauloi*, "mauvaises gens" désignait les vicieux.' In the whole passage, with the exception of lines 11–13, they take Aristotle to describe the incontinent. His use of the word *mochthēria*, which in book VII denotes vice in the strict sense, should not fool us, they say: it is used here in a capacious, loose sense. They criticize Stewart for insisting that already in line 1166b3, *phauloi* denotes akratics, since two lines on, at b5, the expression '*komidēi phauloi*' denotes the radically vicious.

[81] Grönroos (2015) proposes a persuasive account which 'makes the short characterisation in lines 8–11 rather than the discussion of the bad person in lines 11–14 the exception from the main topic'. On Grönroos' analysis, the analysis unfolds as follows: 'Aristotle starts the account by referring to inferior people in general as being conflicted. He then, on line 5, specifies bad people as a particular kind of inferior people, namely as those that are entirely inferior (*hoi komidēi phauloi*). He only then, on line 8, gives the case of the akratic person as a comparison (*hoion*), and fleshes out this case in the following three lines. The acratic conflict consists in going against

Nothing Aristotle says in VII indicates that the vicious experience the happy, global harmony between reason and passion that he takes to be a hallmark of virtue. Aristotle can uphold the distinction between vice and temperance that he drew up in book VII while still maintaining that the lives of vicious agents are rife with pain and regret, only not the kind of regret that akratics feel when they regain their knowledge. Regret – *metameleia* – is any painful, negative assessment of one's past act, where the agent wishes that things were not as they are. But this does not by itself demand that the object of their regret is the property or properties because of which the act is vicious or bad. In other words, regret does not require true beliefs about the good and the bad. Nor does regret entail an acknowledgement that one is to blame for what one did. It is worth recalling that Aristotle also uses *metameleia* to describe the attitude of agents who are not blameworthy for their past acts.[82] Indeed, whether or not the agent is pained determines whether they are excused. At *EN* III.1 1110b19–21, Aristotle distinguishes the non-voluntary and the involuntary by noting that 'everything caused by ignorance is nonvoluntary, but what is involuntary also involves pain and regret'. In other words, only the agent who is pained on the discovery of the facts, and regrets the action that she did because of non-culpable ignorance, can claim to have acted involuntarily (*akōn*). But what is involuntary is not blameworthy, and so she cannot and should not feel *remorse*. This is not an argument for thinking that those who harm others as a result of non-culpable ignorance should blame themselves, but rather that they will regret the harm they caused to others as a result of their ignorance. This shows that Aristotle's use of *metameleia* covers a wider set of cases than repentance and remorse, which require a negative evaluation of one's own act *as blameworthy by the standards of virtue*. Consequently, we should not take Aristotle's use of the term in IX.4 to entail that the bad agent recognizes that his acts are base.

3.6 Regret and Rationalisation

Readers who take *EN* IX.4 to concern the vicious have proposed different ways of making sense of Aristotle's remarks. Irwin suggests that the vicious experience conflict because they do not value their actions as fine; they value their own actions only to the extent that they secure pleasure and benefit. When that

what one believes to be good for oneself, and instead going for what one believes to be harmful (8–10). But after this comparison, from line 11 onwards, he returns to his main concern, which is to elucidate what it is that makes the conflicted *bad* person miserable' (p. 149).

[82] I here disagree with Warren's (2022) assessment of *metameleia* and his appeal to Williams' influential theory of agent regret (see Williams 1981). Warren (2022) attributes a theory of agent regret to Aristotle, though he notes (p. 17, n. 9) that Williams never ties his notion explicitly to *EN* III.1 or to any other Aristotelian text. I think Williams' silence is apt. Grönroos (2015) translates *metameleia* as 'remorse', which makes Aristotle's argument in III.1 incoherent.

objective isn't met, they regret their actions and wish they hadn't done them. By contrast, the virtuous think their acts have value even when they fail to secure the external aim.[83]

Irwin's explanation of the psychological conflict has a desirable level of generality. It is not obvious, however, that it fits every vice equally well. The ostentatious man may seem *excessively* concerned with fine action, to the point where he overspends on public goods, though his notion of the fine is warped. The same could be said for a rash soldier, who may think of glory as fine, and that it is worth taking great risks in the pursuit of victory, even when a brave man would call him foolhardy. I have already noted that Aristotle thinks that 'each state of character has its own distinctive [view of] what is fine and pleasant'. The excellent person is far superior 'because he sees what is true in each case, being himself a sort of standard and measure' (*EN* III.4 1113a32–b3), not because he, unlike others, cares about the fine. It is furthermore not obvious how the vicious would be 'torn to pieces' on Irwin's reconstruction of Aristotle's argument in IX.4. As we have seen, Aristotle thinks that the soul of the vicious person is in conflict (*stasiadzei gar autōn hē psuchē*): 'Because he is vicious one part is distressed at being restrained, and another is pleased [by the intended action]; and so each part pulls (*helkei*) in a different direction, as though they were tearing him apart' (*EN* IX.4 1166b21–3). But retrospective regret at acts that didn't turn out the way you wanted won't explain why your soul is torn apart *before or during* the action.

Irwin thinks that the difference between the virtuous and the vicious is that the former, but not the latter, can value their own acts even when they fail to secure their external objective, since their acts have intrinsic value as fine. But vicious agents, no less than virtuous ones, can be concerned (albeit confusedly) with the fine. Brickhouse's (2003) account seems better suited to make sense of these claims, for he maintains that the mental conflict Aristotle has in mind is due to the fact that the libertine or glutton who pursues sensuous gratification on principle will sometimes have reason to postpone gratification or to forgo pleasures now for the sake of greater enjoyment later. His pursuit of pleasure is governed by reason, and isn't willy-nilly, insofar as he thinks he ought to maximize pleasure in his life as a whole and engages in deliberation to secure the maximal satisfaction of his desires. In this respect, the completely vicious man differs from the one who merely lapses into indulgence. However, argues Brickhouse, once the intemperate man's appetites have grown large and strong (*megalai kai sphodrai*, *EN* III.12 1119b10), they drive out reason by

[83] Irwin (2001). Irwin's 1988 account differs in important respects from his 2001 analysis, but it is the one Brickhouse (2003) rejects.

overpowering his rational plan for the orderly satisfaction of his desires (Brickhouse 2003, esp. pp. 19–21).

My interpretation of IX.4 agrees with Brickhouse in seeing the source of the problem in the principle that the intemperate adopt. But it would be strange if the vicious fled from themselves and 'destroyed themselves' simply because they were unable to stick with an orderly plan for the satisfaction of their desires. I doubt anyone has ever been brought to the brink of suicide because they ruined their appetite through indulging in too many hors d'oeuvres. Here, the appropriate reactive attitude would be anger with oneself for lacking the cleverness required to get the most enjoyment out of life. In other words, the defect would be a logistical failure or a failure of implementation rather than a character flaw. Aristotle claims that vicious men 'shun themselves' and 'seek others to pass their days with'. When they are by themselves, they 'remember many disagreeable actions', he says, and 'anticipate others in the future', but they 'manage to forget these when they are in other people's company' (*EN* IX.4 1166b15–19). This attitude fits more vices than simply intemperance. The coward will not recall running away with pleasure or pride, but may rationalize the action by inventing reasons why saving his own skin was justified.[84] The buffoon thinks telling offensive jokes is justified, but may still feel slightly queasy when they catch a glimpse of their victim's pain. They act contrary to the common good, and thereby alienate those around them. Only a solitary person would not at some level be aware of the consequences of vicious behaviour.

It therefore seems plausible that base people will suffer regrets and that they may even be torn as they act, despite rationalizing the behaviour as needed to secure the life they want. They are horrified, for instance, and shun themselves, when they realize that their pursuit of sex has led them to sleep with underage prostitutes, or when they find themselves shooting up in a crack house in New York, despite their aristocratic bearings (cf. Patrick Melrose, the protagonist of Edward St Aubyn's *Bad News*). Or they recoil in horror when they see their own reflection in a mirror after eating and purging or drinking and getting sick. All the while, they insist that a happy life consists in living precisely as they see fit, consequences be damned. They may find the sources of pleasure contrary to their own conception of themselves as masterly, courageous, and manly – that is, contrary to their ideal of the 'real man'. But although such negative self-assessments employ normative vocabulary, and reflect their view of the fine, it is not akin to moral regret. It's not the underage prostitute the vicious care about when they fail to live up to their own ideals, but themselves.[85]

---

[84] As Barney (2020) persuasively argues.

[85] Müller (2015) attributes what we may call an 'asymmetry thesis' about virtue and vice to Aristotle: while the virtuous' pursuit of the good is principled, the vicious' pursuit of what is

When Aristotle claims that vice destroys the principle of action, he does not claim that the vicious lack a conception of the good that they seek to organize their life around. The question is rather what we are left with when a good principle is destroyed – a bad principle or no principle at all.

For Aristotle, vice is ignorance in the decision, precisely because the decision articulates the agent's conception of the good. Like Socrates, Aristotle thinks that a certain kind of ignorance explains vice, but unlike Socrates, he takes us to be responsible for having false beliefs about the end and making particular decisions based on it. The emotions of the vicious fail to hit the mean because they are not guided by right reason (*orthos logos*), in the sense of reason that *reaches a good*, but rather by what we may call 'wrong reason', which makes them attain a great evil (*kakon mega*, *EN* VI.8 1142a20). The vicious cultivate inappropriate affective attitudes in themselves because they think these attitudes are right. And they think they are right, in part, because they have lived their lives in pursuit of such ends.

3.7 Aristotle's Debt to Plato

Rachel Barney has recently revived the view that scholars who seek to align Aristotle's description of bad people in IX.4 and earlier books are trying to impose order where Aristotle is in fact speaking of different people. According to Barney (2020), it's significant that Aristotle does not call the bad man he describes in IX.4 vicious (*kakos*), but instead describes him in turn as *mochthēros* or *phaulos*:

> This passage is, in my view, simply impossible to square with what Aristotle says about the bad person elsewhere, despite the heroic attempts of recent scholars. My inference is that it is not about the bad person at all; and it is a striking feature of the passage that nowhere does the word *kakos* or any cognate occur. Rather the discussion weaves back and forth between two other groups: the *phauloi* (a group evidently including *all* the non-virtuous 'many', and explicitly including akratics, 1166b8) and the *mochthēroi* (apparently a subset of the *phauloi* who have committed wicked and criminal acts). How either group relates to the *kakoi* properly speaking is an interesting and non-obvious question – one which Aristotle, in avoiding his technical term, is apparently seeking to duck. (Barney 2020, p. 276)[86]

bad is unprincipled. On Müller's reading, the vicious person lives his life willy-nilly, at the mercy of his non-rational desires. I respond to Müller in Nielsen (2017).

86 As Barney (2020) notes, the same terminology is used in the *EE* parallel passage VII.6 1240b11–18. Barney is here reviving the interpretation of Gauthier and Jolif (1970; see their note ad 1166b6–7).

Barney thinks the vignette '*mochthēroi*' is used in XI.4 to depict the non-vicious doers of wicked deeds: agents who do bad acts, but not from a vicious disposition (*hexis*). They are bad along some parameter, and so have a vice or two, but decent along others (e.g. they are intemperate, but not unjust, cowardly, or vain). If so, the *mochthēroi* and *phauloi* are not vicious simpliciter (*kakoi*), though they have some vices.[87] This proposal would make the passage an outlier: Aristotle uses *mochthēros* as a synonym for *kakos* elsewhere (as the relevant entries in Bonitz's (1870) Index Aristotelicum reveal). The claim that he uses the terms in a loose sense in IX.4 is motivated by the assumption that we could otherwise not square the arguments of books VII and IX, and as such, it is ad hoc. But, as I have argued, the passages are compatible if we don't treat all regret as moral regret and all conflict as akratic conflict. In the discussion of justice, injustice, and the voluntary in *EN* V.8 (1135b17–25), *kakos*, *mochthēros*, and *ponēros* are used to refer to the unjust person, who decides on unjust acts. Aristotle here distinguishes between those who do unjust acts coincidentally, and those who do unjust acts because of a previous decision (*prohairesis*) – only the latter are vicious. Here, *kakos/kakia* is picked up by *mochthēros/mochthēria* and *poneros/ponēria* within the scope of a few lines, in a passage where Aristotle is at pains to draw very fine distinctions. It is true that *phaulos* is sometimes used 'to deprecate the ordinary non-virtuous masses' (Barney 2020, p. 276, n. 12 citing *EN* II.3 1104b21; *EN* IV.3 1123b35; *EN* IV.9 1128b25; *EE* VII.2 1238a33). But on closer scrutiny, the evidence suggests Aristotle is in fact speaking about vice in several of the passages Barney cites.[88]

If Barney's construal were right, she would face a dilemma. Aristotle would either maintain in IX.4 that the ordinary non-virtuous masses suffered such horrific mental distress as a result of their ordinary flaws that they 'hate and shun life because of their vice and destroy themselves' – that is, they commit suicide. Alternatively, she would need to distinguish hoi polloi from these people, who have done many terrible acts; but that just is conceding that IX.4 concerns people who are thoroughly bad, and so her claim that the passage is 'not about the bad person at all' is disproved. When Aristotle maintains that the vicious man's soul is torn apart by the conflict between reason and uncontrolled appetite, and that 'even if he cannot be distressed and pleased at the same time, he is soon distressed because he was pleased, and wishes these things had not become

[87] Barney (2020) maintains that vices can exist piecemeal: it is possible to have one vice without having others. Against this, vice in one domain typically causes us to do bad acts in multiple domains. And since justice in general consists in possessing all the virtues, it follows that any agent who possesses as much as one special vice will be unjust in the general, if not the specific sense (cf. *EN* V 1–2).

[88] In *EN* II.3, 1104b21, Aristotle is explicitly discussing vice, as the reference to *kakia* in the conclusion of the passage at b30 reveals: *phauloi* and *kakoi* here pick out the same people.

pleasant to him' (*EN* IX.4 1166b23–5), he is not describing your ordinary non-virtuous person, but someone at the mercy of his uncontrolled appetites. Aristotle's analysis of vice is closer to Plato's analysis of the tormented tyrant than some readers have allowed.

I believe the best way of interpreting Aristotle's remarks about vice in IX.4 is to read them in the context of his discussion of intemperance in book III. Aristotle here suggests that the unrestrained man will end up disappointed *even if he gets what he desires*. For as Aristotle emphasizes, if the appetitive part is not obedient and subordinate to reason by observing due measure in its pursuits, the agent's desire for the pleasant will be 'insatiable' and will seek 'indiscriminate satisfaction' (*EN* IV.12 1119b4–5). Furthermore, the 'active exercise of appetite increases appetite he already had from birth', and so his desire will be insatiable (b7–8). By giving licence to his non-rational part, so that his appetites grow large and intense, the *akolastos* may end up 'dethroning' his rational part so that rational calculation is 'expelled' (*ton logismon ekkrouousin*, b11).[89] The libertine who initially adopts Callicles' maxim 'I will allow my appetites to grow as large as possible and not restrain them (*hōs megistas einai kai mē koladzein*)' (*Gorg*. 492a) will eventually find himself frustrated: his appetites keep growing, and so what seemed sufficient yesterday will no longer do. Even if he deliberates to ensure that he maximizes the amount of pleasure he enjoys in his life as a whole, correcting for distortions of perspective and making what seem like the right trade-offs between pleasures and pains, the sense of control is illusory, for since he simultaneously allows his appetites to grow large and strong, demand will always outstrip supply. By indulging, he will experience diminishing returns. What starts as a principled attempt to enlarge one's appetites as much as possible thus ends up with appetites that can never be sated by any provision. What seems good to the intemperate man is the maximal satisfaction of maximal desires, but following this 'maxi–max' plan yields minimal returns. The more he reaches the first-order objects of pursuit, the less he achieves the ultimate object of his wish (*boulēsis*): to be happy. Thus, what he wants he cannot get, and the increasingly desperate pursuit of satisfaction will lead him to do acts that make him feel ashamed because they contravene his own conception of what is admirable and fine – witness Thrasymachus' blushing in *Republic* 350d when he is defeated in argument.

[89] The end point of this process is bestiality – non-human vice: Phalaris roasting his enemies in a bronze bull. In such cases, the rational principle is missing from the soul altogether, and the sufferer has literally turned into a beast. In the *Republic*, Plato likens the tyrannical soul, completely dominated by appetites, to a werewolf, since he has acquired a taste for human blood.

Once he realizes that restraining appetite is the only way to get what he wants, it is too late. Therefore, neither average base people, like the many, who at some level or at some point approve of themselves and think they are decent, nor those whom Aristotle calls 'utterly base people' (*hoi komidēi phauloi*, *EN* IX.4 1166b5), who have a harder time maintaining the illusion, are psychologically unified, for what they want is not what they get when they pursue pleasant things that are harmful.

Whether this realization only occurs at some time after action, as Aristotle goes on to suggest when he notes that even if they 'cannot be distressed and pleased at the same time, still he is soon distressed because he was pleased, and wishes these things had not become pleasant to him', or whether the conflict is rather apparent right under the surface all the way through action, Aristotle here insists that vice leads to regret, for 'base people are full of regret' (*EN* IX.4 1166b25–6). This is not the kind of regret that the *akratēs* experiences, however, for the *akratēs* regrets the action that he has done since he has the right principle. The content of his *prohairesis*, if not its strength, is right. Therefore, the akratic will suffer from a moral hangover when he recovers from his temporary inattention to his own principles. The intemperate vicious man is not unaware of his own principles as he acts. Initially, his regret is frustration. It is only when he is driven to pursue more and more extreme sources of pleasure to experience the same 'kick' or intensity of pleasure that he starts enjoying actions that even the intemperate think are beyond the pale.[90] And this may lead him to curse the appetites that drive him on and on, however much he has cultivated them deliberately, and however much he thinks they ought to be satisfied. The nature of the principle adopted by the intemperate man, coupled with the boundless nature of sensuous desire, means that his appetite will never be sated. In this regard, Aristotle's image of appetite is Platonic: it's simply the nature of appetite to want more and more and to never be fully sated. The intemperate person, who lacks restraint, will therefore want one thing (the maximal satisfaction of his desires) and get frustrated, since his desires will grow and lead him to pursue pleasure in ways that strike him as shameful and base. When he realizes what he has become, it is too late, and reason will fight a losing battle to keep appetites in check. His sources of pleasure no longer conform to his ideal of a man, no matter how warped that ideal is.

This explains why the intemperate agent should be torn apart by a conflict between a part that is pained at being restrained and a part that is pleased at the intended action. We can understand Aristotle's claims if we recall that wish

[90] I here agree with Brickhouse (2003) that Aristotle may intend a developmental account of (*akolastic*) vice as involving subsequent stages of depravity, depending on the lengths to which the vicious person will go to satisfy his appetites.

(*boulēsis*), as he describes it, is ultimately for the good, not for what appears good to us (cf. *EN* III.4). It is an objective fact that the tyrant will be harmed by his choices, and Plato has painted a striking picture of his suffering. In this regard, then, Aristotle is heir to Plato's conception of vice. Doing as you please will never make you happy unless you know what to want. Once the base man's appetites grow large and strong, it is too late to resist.[91]

3.8 Vices of Thought

I have argued that vice, just like virtue, essentially involves a rational principle. In *Nicomachean Ethics* VI.12 and 13, Aristotle defends the reciprocity of virtue of character and virtue of thought: we cannot have virtue of character without prudence, or prudence without virtue of character. We can now see why Aristotle thinks that all character states involve both the rational and the non-rational parts of soul. While having excessive, deficient, or base desires and emotions is enough to make us do vicious acts, we only count as vicious agents if we do these acts from a vicious state. And acting from a vicious state means acting on a decision that encapsulates one's ignorance of the good. It is therefore a mistake to treat vice as a flaw only of the non-rational part of the soul. The agent is vicious, not simply because he has excessive or deficient appetites and emotions, but also because his rational part is wrong about the kinds of things that promote living well in general. And so, just as Aristotle's definition of virtue of character already entails that it presupposes prudence, character vice cannot exist without what we might call 'imprudence', a state of the rational part whereby we are ignorant about the human good.[92] Aristotle importantly does not adopt this label in the *Nicomachean Ethics*. But his argument needs it.

In *EN* VI.9, Aristotle returns to the need for a 'true supposition' – the right conception of the end. The same point is made at VI.5 1140b31, where Aristotle

---

[91] It is helpful to consider the opposite vice of *akolasia*, which Aristotle claims is rarely found in humans, the nameless vice which he dubs insensitivity (*anaisthēsia*, *EN* III.11 1119a5ff.). Would Aristotle's account of the conflicts of the vicious agent also extend to the insensitive person, who enjoys bodily pleasure too little? Consider the anorectic. Convinced that the good life consists in not gaining weight, the anorectic adopts thinness as an overarching end. Initially, all is well. But over time, the anorectic experiences the harmful consequences of not eating. Even as their body weakens and their social bonds start fraying, the anorectic remains fully psychologically committed to not gaining weight. The anorectic is thus conflicted, just like their counterpart, the *akolastos*, and is full of regrets. All the same, the false commitment to being thin persists. (It is an open question whether Aristotle is correct to classify deficient enjoyment of bodily pleasure as a vice. The border between vice and disease seems less than clear-cut).

[92] Aristotle defines prudence as a 'state grasping the truth (*hexis alēthēs*), involving reason, concerned with action about things that are good or bad for a human being (*peri ta anthopōi agatha kai kaka*)' and says that its end is acting well itself (*eupraxia*) (VI.5, 1140b5–8). And he says that the prudent person deliberates finely about things that promote living well in general (*to eu zēn holōs*, VI.5 1140a28).

identifies having the right supposition with having the right principle (*archē*) and acting for the sake of the right end. Prudence, he argues in VI.9, involves good deliberation (*euboulia*), insofar as good deliberation 'is the type of correctness that accords with what is expedient for promoting the end about which prudence is true supposition' (*hupolēpsis*, VI.9 1142b33–6).[93] Imprudence (the state by which we adopt false beliefs about ends) would consequently not be a lack of cleverness in planning one's life as a whole, but rather a failure to know and be guided by the right supposition about the end in one's deliberation. Although the vicious person may be eminently skilled in finding means to ends, whether instrumental or constitutive, that merely makes matters worse.[94]

Strikingly, Aristotle never develops an account of vices of thought in *Nicomachean Ethics* VI. Nor does he refer to such vices as anything other than absence of virtue in the discussion in the *Ethics*.[95] Perhaps the only indication that he had the outline of a positive concept is the stray references to *aphrosunē* ('folly') in *EN* VII.2 1146a27 and 1149a5. The fool, Aristotle argues, has the wrong ends, as can be seen by his response to a sophistical puzzle: 'A certain argument, then, concludes that foolishness combined with incontinence makes someone act contrary to what he supposes [is right], but since he supposes that good things are bad and that it is wrong to do them, he will do the good actions, not the bad' (*EN* VII.2 1146a27; note the reference to *hupolambanein*, the verb from which *huplēpsis* is derived). Here, *aphrosunē* is a state that makes us aim at bad ends. Had Aristotle developed a positive account of vices of thought in book VI, he would likely not have positioned virtues of thought in a mean between two vices, but would have explained how vices of thought, as the converse of their correlative virtues, are 'false states', that is, states that make us believe falsehoods about the human good. As such, vices of thought would not simply be failures of practical reasoning but would crucially involve the adoption of false supposition about the human good and the unqualified end of human action.

To be virtuous, we need good deliberation, practical perception of particulars, and the right conception of the end. Practical perception is of no use if it is not

---

93 I here take 'about which' to refer back to 'the end' rather than the less plausible 'what is expedient for promoting the end'. For a defence of the latter reading, see Moss (2011, p. 230–1).

94 Aristotle says in *EN* VI.12 that cleverness, as the capacity to do the actions that tend to promote whatever goal is assumed and to attain them, is praiseworthy if the goal is fine, but if the goal is base, it is unscrupulousness (1144a26–9). The opposite of *euboulia* (*dusboulia*?) is the state whereby deliberation makes us reach an evil, even when we are deliberating about constituents of the (bad) end we have assumed.

95 In *EN* VII.5 1149a10, Aristotle claims that some foolish people lack reason altogether, and live only by sense-perception, for instance 'some races of distant foreigners' [sic]. These are not the foolish people who have bad principles, however.

informed by the right conception. That is why Aristotle associates ignorance in the decision with ignorance about a universal, and why a failure to perceive the right particulars at the right time and in the right way leads to *akrasia* rather than vice. Had Aristotle included a more elaborate definition of vice as a state of character, it might have included a reference to imprudence, just as his definition of virtue of character includes a reference to prudence (since the mean, as Aristotle states, is defined 'by reference to reason, that is to say, to the reason by reference to which the prudent person would define it' (*EN* II.7 1107a2–3)). Perhaps, then, we may infer that vice, as Aristotle conceives of it, is a 'state that decides, consisting in a deficient or excessive extreme, extremes relative to us', where the *actual* extremes are defined 'by reference to reason, that is to say, to the reason by reference to which the *prudent* person would define them', but where the *perceived* mean pursued by the *imprudent* person is in fact identical to one of the extremes. The *imprudent* person thus suffers from ignorance in the decision, and if he gets what he wants, he will have got himself a great evil. As Socrates remarks, 'what else is misery than desiring bad things and securing them?' (*Meno* 78a6).

References

Primary Sources

I use the Oxford Classical Texts editions of Plato and Aristotle.

Translations are taken from:

Aristotle (1984). *Complete Works*. Barnes, J. (ed.). Princeton, NJ: Princeton University Press.

Aristotle (1995). *Aristotle: Selections*. Irwin, T. H. and Fine, G. (tr.). Indianapolis, IN: Hackett.

Aristotle (1999). *Nicomachean Ethics*, 2nd ed. Irwin, T. H. (tr.). Indianapolis, IN: Hackett.

Aristotle (2011). *The Eudemian Ethics*. Kenny, A. (tr.). Oxford: Oxford University Press.

Plato (1997). *Complete Works*. Cooper, J. (ed.). Indianapolis, IN: Hackett.

Unless otherwise noted, other translations are taken from relevant volumes of the Loeb Classical Library.

Secondary Sources

Annas, J. (1977). Plato and Aristotle on Friendship and Altruism. *Mind* 86, 432–54.

Annas, J. (1993). *The Morality of Happiness*. Oxford: Oxford University Press.

Annas, J. (2017). *Virtue and Law in Plato and Beyond*. Oxford: Oxford University Press.

Arruzza, C. (2019). *A Wolf in the City: Tyranny and the Tyrant in Plato's* Republic. New York: Oxford University Press.

Barney, R. (2020). Becoming Bad: Aristotle on Vice and Moral Habituation. *Oxford Studies in Ancient Philosophy* 57, 273–308.

Bonitz, H. (1870). *Index Aristotelicus*. Berlin: Georg Reimer.

Brickhouse, T. (2003). Does Aristotle Have a Consistent Account of Vice? *Review of Metaphysics* 57, 3–23.

Brink, D. (2021). *Fair Opportunity and Responsibility*. Oxford: Oxford University Press.

Broadie, S. (1991). *Ethics with Aristotle*. Oxford: Oxford University Press.

Broadie, S. and Rowe, C. (2002). *Aristotle Nicomachean Ethics*. Oxford: Oxford University Press.

Crisp, R. (1998). *Routledge Philosophy Guidebook to Mill on Utilitarianism*. London: Routledge.

Dirlmeier, F. (1960). *Aristoteles Nikomachische Ethik.* Berlin: Akademie Verlag.

Foot, P. (2001). *Natural Goodness*. Oxford: Clarendon Press.

Gauthier, R. A. and Jolif, J. Y. (1970). *L'Éthique à Nicomaque*, 2nd ed. Paris: Publications Universitaires.

Gerber, D. E. (ed. and trans.) (1999). *Greek Iambic Poetry: From the Seventh to the Fifth Centuries BC*. Cambridge, MA: Harvard University Press.

Grant, A. (1866). *The Ethics of Aristotle*, two vols. London: Longmans, Green & Co.

Grönroos, G. (2015). Why Is Aristotle's Vicious Person Miserable? In Rabbås, Ø. (ed.), *The Quest for the Good Life*. Oxford: Oxford University Press, 146–63.

Gwynn, W. B. (1991). Cruel Nero: The Concept of the Tyrant and the Image of Nero in Western Political Thought. *History of Political Thought* 12 (3), 421–55.

Hampson, M. (2021). Aristotle and the Necessity of Habituation: Re-reading *Nicomachean Ethics* 2.4. *Phronesis* 66 (1), 1–26.

Hitz, Z. (2010). Degenerate Regimes in Plato's *Republic*. In McPherran, M. (ed.), *Plato's Republic: A Critical Guide*. Cambridge: Cambridge University Press, 103–31.

Hobbes, T. (1996). *Leviathan*. Tuck, R. (ed.). Cambridge: Cambridge University Press.

Hoekstra, K. (2015). Hobbes's Thucydides. In Martinich, A. P. and Hoekstra, K. (eds.), *The Oxford Handbook of Hobbes*. Oxford: Oxford University Press, 547–74.

Irwin, T. H. (1988). *Aristotle's First Principles*. Oxford: Clarendon Press.

Irwin, T. H. (1995). *Plato's Ethics*. Oxford: Oxford University Press.

Irwin, T. H. (2001). Vice and Reason. *Journal of Ethics* 5, 73–97.

Jimenez, M. (2016). Aristotle on Becoming Virtuous by Doing Virtuous Acts. *Phronesis* 61 (1), 3–32.

Kamtekar, R. (2017). *Plato's Moral Psychology: Intellectualism, the Divided Soul, and Desire for Good*. Oxford: Oxford University Press.

Kontos, P. (2018). Radical Evil in Aristotle's Ethics and Politics. In Kontos, P. (ed.), *Evil in Aristotle*. Cambridge: Cambridge University Press, 75–97.

Kraut, R. (2002). *Aristotle: Political Philosophy.* Oxford: Oxford University Press.

Larivée, A. (2012). Eros Tyrannos: Alcibiades as the Model of the Tyrant in Book IX of the *Republic*. *International Journal of the Platonic Tradition*, 6 (1), 1–26.

Lockwood, T. (2020). Acting Finely the Role of the King (*Politics* 5.11.1314a40). Unpublished paper presented at the meeting of the American Philosophical Association Central Division, 28 February 2020.

Marshall, L. A. (2017). Gadfly or Spur? The Meaning of *muōps* in Plato's *Apology* of Socrates. *Journal of Hellenic Studies* 137, 163–74.

Mill, J. S. (1863). *Utilitarianism*. London: Parker, Son, and Bourn.

Moss, J. (2011). Virtue Makes the Goal Right: Virtue and Phronesis in Aristotle's Ethics. *Phronesis* 56, 204–61.

Müller, J. (2015). Aristotle on Vice. *British Journal of the History of Philosophy* 23 (3), 459–77.

Müller, J. (2018). Practical and Productive Thinking in Aristotle. *Phronesis* 63 (2), 148–75.

Nielsen, K. M. (2017). Vice in the *Nicomachean Ethics*. *Phronesis* 62 (1), 1–25.

Nielsen, K. M. (2019). The Tyrant's Vice: Pleonexia and Lawlessness in Plato's *Republic*. *Philosophical Perspectives* 33, 146–69.

Nielsen, K. M. (2022). Deliberation and Decision in the *Eudemian Ethics*. In Di Basilio, G. (ed.), *Essays on Aristotle's Eudemian Ethics*. New York: Routledge, 80–100.

Nightingale, A. W. (1999). Plato's Lawcode in Context: Rule by Written Law in Athens and Magnesia. *Classical Quarterly* 49 (1), 100–22.

Pearson, G. (2018). Aristotle on Psychopathology. In Kontos, P. (ed.), *Evil in Aristotle*. Cambridge: Cambridge University Press, 122–49.

Penner, T. (1991). Desire and Power in Socrates. *Apeiron* 24, 147–202.

Reeve, C. D. C. (2012). *Blindness and Reorientation in Plato's Republic*. Oxford: Oxford University Press.

Rogers, B (1999). *A. J. Ayer: A Life*. London: Chatto & Windus.

Rowe, C. (2020). Plato on *Kakia* in Some Later Dialogues. In Veillard, C., Renaut, O., and El Murr, D. (eds.), *Les philosophes face au vice, de Socrate à Augustin*, *Philosophia Antiqua* (special issue) 154, 95–113.

Sayre-McCord, G. (2011). Mill's 'Proof' of the Principle of Utility: A More than Half-Hearted Defense. *Social Philosophy & Policy* 18, 330–60.

Schofield, M. (2011). Aristotle and the Democratization of Politics. In Morison, B. and Ierodiakonou, K. (eds.), *Episteme, etc.: Essays in Honour of Jonathan Barnes*. Oxford: Oxford University Press, 285–301.

Scott, D. (2000). Plato's Critique of the Democratic Character. *Phronesis* 45 (1), 19–37.

Scott, D. (2006). *Plato's Meno*. Cambridge: Cambridge University Press.

Scott, D. (2020). *Listening to Reason in Plato and Aristotle*. Oxford: Oxford University Press.

Stewart, J. A. (1892). *Notes on the Nicomachean Ethics*, two vols. Oxford: Clarendon Press.

Strauss Clay, J. (1986). Archilochus and Gyges: An Interpretation of Fr. 23 West. *Quaderni Urbinati di Cultura Classica* 24 (3), 7–17.

Warren, J. (2022). *Regret: A Study in Ancient Moral Psychology*. Oxford: Oxford University Press.

Williams, B. (1981). *Moral Luck*. Cambridge: Cambridge University Press.

Acknowledgements

I am pleased to record my gratitude to audiences at the University of Cambridge, King's College London, the University of Oxford, the University of Oslo, University College London, and Paris Nanterre University/University of Paris 1 Panthéon–Sorbonne, and especially to the many graduate students who asked me questions. The editors and anonymous referees of *Phronēsis* and *Philosophical Perspectives* offered important advice, as did an anonymous referee for the *Elements* Series. James Warren, the editor, deserves special thanks for his wisdom and patient stewardship. Section 2 of this Element is an abridged version of Nielsen (2019). Section 3 incorporates parts of Nielsen (2017); I thank the editors and Brill for permissions.

Cambridge Elements ☰

Ancient Philosophy

James Warren
University of Cambridge

James Warren is Professor of Ancient Philosophy at the University of Cambridge. He is the author of *Epicurus and Democritean Ethics* (Cambridge, 2002), *Facing Death: Epicurus and his Critics* (2004), *Presocratics* (2007) and *The Pleasures of Reason in Plato, Aristotle and the Hellenistic Hedonists* (Cambridge, 2014). He is also the editor of *The Cambridge Companion to Epicurus* (Cambridge, 2009), and joint editor of *Authors and Authorities in Ancient Philosophy* (Cambridge, 2018).

About the Series

The Elements in Ancient Philosophy series deals with a wide variety of topics and texts in ancient Greek and Roman philosophy, written by leading scholars in the field. Taking a theme, question, or type of argument, some Elements explore it across antiquity and beyond. Others look in detail at an ancient author, a specific work, or a part of a longer work, considering its structure, content, and significance, or explore more directly ancient perspectives on modern philosophical questions.

Cambridge Elements

Ancient Philosophy

Elements in the Series

Relative Change
Matthew Duncombe

Plato's Ion: Poetry, Expertise, and Inspiration
Franco V. Trivigno

Aristotle on Ontological Priority in the Categories
Ana Laura Edelhoff

The Method of Hypothesis and the Nature of Soul in Plato's Phaedo
John Palmer

Aristotle on Women: Physiology, Psychology, and Politics
Sophia M. Connell

Vice in Ancient Philosophy: Plato and Aristotle on Moral Ignorance and Corruption of Character
Karen Margrethe Nielsen

A full series listing is available at: www.cambridge.org/EIAP

For EU product safety concerns, contact us at Calle de José Abascal, 56–1°,
28003 Madrid, Spain or eugpsr@cambridge.org.

www.ingramcontent.com/pod-product-compliance
Ingram Content Group UK Ltd.
Pitfield, Milton Keynes, MK11 3LW, UK
UKHW022143080726
473066UK00010B/734

* 9 7 8 1 1 0 8 7 1 3 4 3 6 *